The Power of Vibrational Medicine

Healing with the Bioacoustics of Nature

Gretchen Weger Snell, PhD, DNM

Copyright © 2019 Gretchen Weger Snell, PhD, DNM

All rights reserved.

ISBN:
ISBN-13: 9781796297058

Cover art: Vector art by Victoria Field

DEDICATION

This work is dedicated to all the teachers and visionaries who have blazed this trail before me; to those who walk this path with me; those who have supported me during this process; those who make this work possible; to my clients and students who continue to teach me and inspire me daily; to the bright children who are changing the world for the positive; and to the healing of the Earth and all her inhabitants

DISCLAIMER:

The information in this book is not intended to replace professional medical treatment. Consultation and continual treatment with a medical doctor is advised. The tools and philosophies presented in this work are not intended to diagnose or treat disease, rather to present a scientifically credible proposal to bridge both conventional and traditional health care therapies.

CONTENTS

	List of Figures	vi
	Introduction	ix
1	Materializing the Conceptual	1
2	A Quantum Leap	7
3	Bioelectromagnetic and Subtle Energy Fields	11
4	Bioacoustic Frequencies and Sound Therapy	21
5	Tools for Monitoring the Human Energy Field	39
6	The Research Project	63
7	The Results of the Research	73
8	Discussion and Summary	93
9	Conclusions: A Shift in Consciousness	97
	References	102

LIST OF FIGURES

Figure 1 Kirlian Photograph of Acoustic Sounds on Healthy Human Cells, © Fabien Maman 27

Figure 2 Frequency Correspondence Chart © Anthony Fiorenza 32

Figure 3. Incoherent vs. Coherent Heart Rhythm © 2009 Institute of HeartMath 44

Figure 4. Meridians (Source www.sott.net/article/316751) 48

Figure 5. EDA Testing 56

Figure 6 Example of an Indicator Drop Using EAV 59

Figure 7 Electro Dermal Analysis Testing 61

Figure 8 Sample of Individual Coherence Reading - Raw Data 73

Figure 9. Compilation of All Participants, Percentage of Improvement in Autonomic Coherence after One Session 74

Figure 10. Compilation of All Participants, Percentage Improvements in Autonomic Coherence after Two Weeks 75

Figure 11. Compilation of All Participants, Percentage Improvements in Coherence - Totals 76

Figure 12 Sample of HRV Raw Data 77

Figure 13. 1-Minute HRV Deep Breathing Assessment, Combined for All Participants 78

Figure 14 Sample EDA Test Data for Bioacoustic Research Project 80

Figure 15 EDA Results for Participant AE 81

Figure 16 EDA Results for Participant CR 82

Figure 17 EDA Results for Participant KE 82

Figure 18 EDA Results for Participant MF 84

Figure 19 EDA Results for Participant – KD 85

Figure 20 EDA Results for Participant KA 86

Figure 21 EDA Results for Participant PL 87

Figure 22 EDA Results for Participant RS 88

Figure 23 EDA Results for Participant MH 88

INTRODUCTION

What if we have the power to affect our health to a far greater capacity than we've been led to believe? What if we possess an internal language, a system that communicates information and can be directed to positively influence our healing process? How we answer these questions is important as it defines our understanding and approach to healing. This will necessitate a shift in our materialistic approach to medicine to include the discoveries of quantum physics, which redefine frequency as the basis of our physical reality. It will require a re-vision to integrate the wisdom of the traditional forms of energy medicine, inclusive of vibrational medicine, with the technological advances of conventional western medicine. If healing is our ultimate goal, we must create a synthesis of therapies that address the whole of the human condition, to encompass the totality of our being.

Groundbreaking research in the field of medicine demonstrates that regulation and communication within living organisms can no longer be adequately explained through strictly chemical mechanical means. Rather, it is the primacy of electromagnetic frequencies (vibrations) that attenuate cellular receptors facilitating communication within living organisms. Every organ, tissue and cell has its own resonant frequency, which when operating efficiently, work harmoniously together. When this frequency is altered, loss of coherence ensues leading to disease. Hence, providing the correct or 'healthy' frequencies often can restore balance through entraining the oscillations back to coherence. This opens the possibility for vibrational medicine, in the form of sound and bioacoustic harmonics, as an option for restoring the natural balance.

To understand the science that underlies the mechanism for this communication lies in knowledge of a tissue system that until recently has been vastly ignored by western medicine, the Extra Cellular Matrix (ECM). Comprehensive data and information from years of research in ECM is detailed in *The Extracellular Matrix and Ground Regulation: Basis for Holistic Biological Medicine* (Pischinger) and *Energy Medicine: The Scientific Basis* (Oschman). The ECM is a highly structural, electrically charged semiconducting liquid crystal gel that maintains contact with every organ and cell in the body. Signals in the form of electromagnetic frequencies are conducted through this tissue. Vibrational patterns, i.e. electromagnetic frequencies, consistent with health introduced to the body are transmitted through the ECM. These electromagnetic signals attenuate the cellular receptors, tissue and organs with which the specific pattern resonates. Like a tuning fork, the cells will then resonate with the frequency consistent with optimal functioning. Once attenuated energetically, changes are stimulated to chemically up regulate or down regulate processes for support assimilation, regeneration, elimination and repair.

Unquestionably, nutrient deficiencies and toxic debris must be addressed to support the physical foundation so electrical conduction of electromagnetic signals can be maximally efficient. As is presented in the data (pg.50), this is an area in which Electro Dermal Analysis can be an exceedingly important adjunct to practice of medicine. This technology (EDA) allows for the analysis of the conductance of the electromagnetic frequencies through the cells, tissue, organs and organ systems. Numerous scientific studies and clinical data prove a correlation for signal conduction and health of the tissue.

One of the main roadblocks in accepting the viability of energy medicine, lies in the challenge of demonstrating its beneficial effects through observable and measurable means. Although the recognition and manipulation of energy systems of the body has been fundamental to healing systems for numerous cultures around the globe, conventional Western medicine still dismisses them as mystical or supernatural, within the realm of pseudoscience. Cultures have thrived since antiquity and into modern day through the incorporation of subtle energies in their system of healing. However, the prevailing belief remains that results of vibrational therapies are subjective, and without objective measurement fall outside the realm of science. With advanced technology we are now able to detect and observe the presence of the subtle energies that have been previously undetectable by conventional methods.

This work presented in this book is based on the assertion that illness is initiated by imbalances in the energy systems of the body and proposes that methods to detect and to correct these imbalances are integral to a comprehensive health system. The innovative research discussed in this work illustrates methods for both analysis of these imbalances and proposes a form of vibrational therapy (bioacoustics harmonics) to correct these imbalances. The results of this research illustrate that detectable changes do occur on an energetic level, often prior to physical manifestation. The project discussed in this book demonstrates that the beneficial effects of energy medicine in the form of specific targeted bioacoustic harmonics can be observed through objective measurements - the biomarkers of autonomic nervous system coherence, heart rate variability and meridian analysis. Established research proves that improvement in any of these variables positively impacts a wide variety of parameters consistent with positive health. Considering the results of this research, it is the opinion of the author that a comprehensive medical system calls for analysis of the subtle energy systems as well as the physical body.

****

The healing vocal talent behind the compilation of Sayonic Therapy belongs to Multi-Grammy nominated recording artist, Kate Hart. Sayonic is an ancient word which translates as "the language of frequency". While teaching, she noticed significant changes occurring in students when teaching them to connect to their core voice. Shifts in confidence and health occurred with her students opening a desire to understand how sound may be used as a therapeutic modality. Combined with studies of ancient cultures and writings, Kate discovered frequencies related to deep alignment. The research that is presented in this dissertation was conducted to discover how these frequencies affected the various levels and processes in the body. This unique process is now being trademarked as Sayonic Therapy, and currently being used by individuals, massage therapists, nurses, dentists, naturopaths, cranial sacral therapists and mo

1. MATERIALIZING THE CONCEPTUAL

A few years ago, a colleague asked me to provide the research arm to a healing modality she was developing. She wanted to develop a better understanding of the observed effects that sound therapy was producing in her clients. I volunteered to do an energy analysis in my clinic to help identify the effects.

We shared the philosophy that illness is initiated by imbalances in the body's subtle energy fields; therefore, we believed that this is where we must shift our focus in the healing process. We also knew that to enhance healing a client must take an active role in the process. What began as an effort to develop a therapy that would empower clients to build their health naturally, resulted in a project that has more profound implications for the field of healing. The results provided the foundation for this work.

Years of personal clinical experience has proven that changes which affect the healing process can be detected on an energetic level prior to physical manifestation. Moreover, since these energetic changes remain undetected by conventional diagnostics, they are often deemed subjective and dismissed as being unscientific. I believe we are missing crucial information by ignoring the energy body in our current practice of conventional Western medicine. This project provided an avenue for obtaining objective measurement of the effects of vibrational therapy (sound) on the energy systems of the body, thus changing the discussion regarding scientific validity.

A research project was designed to determine if effects of specific vibrational frequencies could be shown to positively affect biomarkers and dynamic homeostatic mechanisms that promote health. Combinations of numerous frequencies were tested on volunteer subjects to analyze the effects both subjectively and objectively. The frequencies were those found in ancient texts known to align with chakras and meridians, the Solfeggio scale, crystal and Tibetan bowls, mantras, Platonic solids, Rife frequencies and Schumann resonance. As a professional recording artist, my colleague developed and recorded melodic patterns using multi-layered, deep field harmonics using the human voice to produce these frequencies within the range of human hearing. The compilation provided an independent variable in the form of bioacoustic frequencies that allowed me to research the effects in a clinical setting.

The study culminated in the creation of a "bioacoustic homocord", a compilation that mirrors the frequencies of nature to restore measurable peace and balance from which healing can occur. This new modality called Sayonic Therapy (an archaic term for "the Language of Frequency") transcends color or creed, economic or health status to empower an individual to help direct their healing process. The latest discoveries in quantum physics are redefining our understanding that frequency is the basis of physical reality; *that each particle is in its essence a one-dimensional string vibrating with its own music.* Vibrational therapies constitute a means for restoring the balance within the biochemistry as well as the bioenergy of living organisms for building health.

****

Although the discoveries of quantum physics at the beginning of the twentieth century proved that all matter is essentially accumulated energy, the concept of integrating energy in conventional medicine remains a polarizing subject. One of the main difficulties with accepting the viability of energy medicine is the continual challenge to prove its beneficial effects. It is said that results of energy therapies are subjective, and being without objective measurement, these therapies fall outside the realm of science. With advanced technology, we are now able to observe and monitor the presence of the subtle energies that have been previously undetectable by conventional methods (Oschman, 2002, p. 1). The study in this book examined health from the viewpoint that illness is initiated by imbalances in the energy systems of the body and proposed that methods to detect and to correct these imbalances are integral to a comprehensive health system. This work discusses the quantum model of medicine as a framework for understanding the energy system of the body. Quantum medicine provides a scientific basis for validating my conviction that objective analysis of the human bioenergy field should be an essential part of a comprehensive system of healing, providing valuable information often missed with conventional diagnostics.

Advances in conventional medicine over the past century, both pharmaceutical and technological, have saved incalculable human life in acute situations. However, the same cannot be said of chronic diseases as they continue to escalate in modern times. The CDC's own website states that:

Chronic diseases are responsible for 7 of 10 deaths each year, and treating people with chronic diseases accounts for 86% of our nation's health care costs. Chronic diseases and conditions—such as heart disease, stroke, cancer, type 2 diabetes, obesity, and arthritis—are among the most common, costly, and preventable of all health problems.

Half of all American adults have at least one chronic condition, and almost one of three has multiple chronic conditions." ("CDC's Chronic Disease Prevention System," 2017)

As far back as 1937, the recipient of the Nobel Prize in Medicine, Albert Szent-Györgyi stated that, "Most human suffering at present is caused by so-called 'degenerative diseases – the name standing for 'disease we don't understand and consequently can do nothing about." The existence of such a closed group of diseases also points toward a major gap in our basic knowledge...Some fundamental fact, if not a whole dimension, is missing from our biological thinking. (Rosch, 2015, p. 454). It is my belief that the missing dimension is that of the subtle energy forces, at a subatomic level, which is now slowly coming into sharper focus with the application of quantum physics to medicine and healing practices.

Our project proved the proposal that the healing effects of energy medicine in the form of bioacoustic frequencies *can* be objectively measured and monitored using biomarkers of Heart Rate Variability (HRV), autonomic nervous system coherence and acupuncture meridian analysis. Research in the public domain correlates dysfunction of any of these variables with various pathological conditions such as cardiovascular disease and metabolic syndrome, as well as increased levels of anxiety, depression and stress (McCraty, 2015, p.13). The results of the research demonstrate that by using a specific energetic therapy comprising targeted bioacoustic frequencies associated with homeostasis, the effects on the physiological as well as the subtle energy bodies can be monitored and shown to improve the parameters of HRV, autonomic system and meridian coherence. This indicates that this form of energy medicine, i.e. bioacoustic frequencies known as Sayonic Therapy, can be an effective healing method. Moreover, it could be used as an adjunct to other healing therapies as it has been demonstrated to improve parameters known to be associated with self-regulatory capacity and a positive direction of healing.

2. A QUANTUM LEAP

The shift from Newtonian physics that views the world as mechanistic, to an Einsteinian view that recognizes life as a network of complex energy fields, necessitates a revision that includes the dynamics of energy in our healing system. The discoveries of quantum physics help redefine the conventional model with a new understanding of disease and the healing process. A new model of Quantum Medicine is an integrative approach to medicine that expands the current material model to include the subtle energy bodies. Medical doctor Dr. Paul Drouin, and quantum physicist Dr. Amit Goswami, developed a revolutionary model of medicine and healing that integrates both the current material approach based in principles of classical physics, with new discoveries and principles of quantum physics. In his book, *The Quantum Doctor* – Dr. Goswami provides the theoretical framework of how principles of quantum theory are applied to the practice of medicine. Dr. Drouin's book, *Creative Integrative Medicine: A Medical Doctor's Journey toward a New Vision for Health Care,* illustrates how the quantum theory of integrative medicine can be utilized in actual practice with successful examples of healing. His curriculum revises our current framework of conventional practices based on the mechanistic model to include the principles of quantum physics. This novel approach expands our current medical model to integrate the physical and the subtle energy bodies.

One of the corollaries of quantum physics is that we are more than mere observers; but rather we are participating in the conscious creation of our universe. Quantum medicine is rooted in the philosophy that consciousness, rather than matter, is the ground of all being. Not the limited, individuated consciousness of ego, rather a universal consciousness that is a non-local domain of all potentiality. Objects are waves of possibility until they are observed, and whether they are observed as a wave or particle depends on the way in which the event is measured /observed. The paradox of wave/particle duality, defined by quantum mechanics, is resolved by viewing universal consciousness as the ground of potential for both wave and particle. It is the "causal act of choice by consciousness that collapses the waves of possibility into particle of actuality converting them from a many faceted object to a one-faceted one" (Goswami, Reed, & Goswami, 1993, p. 84). The choice represents a "collapse" of the wave potential into particle, that is, the change from possibility into actuality. The events we experience, including our perspective on health or disease, are the result of the causal acts of possible choice of consciousness.

The mechanistic model of conventional medicine sees consciousness as epiphenomena of the physical body and the result of upward causation from elementary particles. In contrast, the Quantum model postulates that a universal consciousness is the ground of all being and that physical matter is produced by downward causation from this universal consciousness as a result of choice. Our choices, or the quantum collapse, arise from the non-local, cosmic consciousness, where we experience ourselves as one with everyone and everything else, rather than the localized ego. In this non-local, cosmic consciousness, the physical as well as the subtle energy bodies exist as possibilities until "collapsed" into manifested experiences of consciousness. Ervin Laszlo echoes this viewpoint in his book, *Science and the Akashic Field*. Laszlo states that the underlying principles in ancient cosmologies are that the existence of things in the physical world are a "distillation of the basic energy of the cosmos, descending from its original source", and that "the physical world is a reflection of the energy vibrations of a more subtle world that, in turn, are reflections of a more subtle energy field. Creation and all subsequent existence is a progression downward and outward from the primordial source" (Laszlo, 2007, p. 103).

The Quantum Model includes the quantum physics principles of non-locality, discontinuity and entanglement.

Non-locality

The term non-local is used to describe an instantaneous transfer of information or energy without the exchange of signals though space-time that is required by classical physics. The quantum model postulates that the subtle bodies and physical bodies are quantum objects existing as waveforms of potential. Since each of the five subtle bodies are correlated quantum objects, a collapse in one level will manifest in all other levels simultaneously, without the local exchange of signals. This provides the basis of the theory of how the five subtle bodies interact or communicate with one another.

Discontinuity

In contrast to classical physics, changes in a quantum system go through a "leap" from one energy state to another without going through steps. When the measurement or conscious choice is made, the possibility waves collapse discontinuously to a localized particle all at once. This quantum leap explains sudden changes, "leaps" in healing, and spontaneous healing. Dr. Drouin calls this sudden insight the "a-ha moment" that represents an abrupt break from the conditioned ego response, which creates new possibilities for healing.

Entanglement

In the quantum model, entanglement underscores the novel idea that both practitioner and client are intricately engaged in the healing process. This process known as a tangled hierarchy is both unique and individualized in contrast to the current conventional model.
Innovative research supports the idea of the living organism being a quantum system that operates according to quantum principles. In her book, *The Rainbow and the Worm; The Physics of Organisms*, Mae Wan Ho describes a living organisms as "quantum coherent exhibiting the properties of quantum superposition (unlimited possibilities in potential), delocation, inseparability and non-local interactions" (Ho, 2008, p. 280). In accordance with Erwin Schrödinger's discovery of quantum entanglement, Ho states that, *"A quantum coherent system has neither space nor time, therefore the collapse of one part is instantaneously communicated to other parts, regardless of how great a distance separates the two"* (Ho, 2008, p. 279). This experimental research by Mae Wan Ho supports the philosophy of the quantum model of medicine, which has been applied to this innovative project.

3. BIOELECTROMAGNETIC AND SUBTLE ENERGY FIELDS

"Misdirected life force is the activity in the disease process. Disease has no energy save what it borrows from the life of the organism. It is by adjusting the life force that healing must be brought about." ~ **Kabbalah**

The concept of energy fields in medicine extends to antiquity, only recently being eclipsed by the development of cell theory, microbiology and pharmacology. As far back as the 3rd Century B.C. the Greek anatomist Galen held the belief that vital spirits (energy) were necessary for life. Hippocrates acknowledged that hidden forces were the healers of disease. According to oldest medical texts, the concept of subtle energy has always been integral to the healing process. In *Avicenna's Medicine: 11th Century Cannon,* we see the idea,

> When the organ function becomes abnormal, there is a problem with its energy, and a problem with the organ's energy causes a disease in the organ...Standard tissue 'pathology' appears relatively late in the process, after the tissues have lost their energetic and metabolic means of responding (or reacting) to the disease and trying to maintain homeostasis and 'normality' (Abu-Asab, Amri, & Micozzi, 2013, p. 19).

The notion of vital force or vital energy has been fundamental to medical philosophies and sacred texts of indigenous cultures around the globe. Vital energy is known as chi in China, Prana in India, Pneuma by the ancient Greeks, Num by the Kalahari and Mana by the people of Hawaii. Modern scientists call it Orgone, Ether, Bioplasmic Energy or the Universal Life Force (Swanson,

2010, Chapter 3). It was recognized that the involvement of this vital energy was an essential component of any healing therapy.

Claude Swanson declares that a scientific revolution is taking place to accommodate our new understanding of energy. His book, *Life Force; the Scientific Basis*, details scientific research in energy medicine from around the world. Perhaps Swanson summarizes one of the most comprehensive definitions of the "Life Force" and the evolving understanding of life energy.

> It is like no other force known to science. It responds to consciousness and alters the other basic laws of physics. It is intimately involved with life processes, and plays a central role in growth and healing. It does not weaken with distance and penetrates most materials and shielding. In many cultures, manipulation of this energy is one of the central arts of medicine…It constitutes a fifth force which has been overlooked by Western physics…It is the 'building energy', which reverses entropy, brings order out of chaos and makes life possible…It creates a bridge between the old paradigm of space-time and a new dimension of reality, which leads to a new model of consciousness and potential unification of science and spirituality (Swanson, 2010, p. 1, 51).

A 1993 article by William Tiller, "*What are Subtle Energies*", identifies subtle energies as "beyond the four fundamental energies that we know and accept", which are strong and weak nuclear forces, electromagnetic and gravitational" (Rosch, 2015, p. 159). Much like the existence of x-rays and gamma rays were completely unknown to man until equipment was developed to detect them. Yet, their effects on matter could be observed. Like the vital energy of the meridians and the chakras, we do not have the means to directly measure them, yet we can observe their effects on the physical realm. The four subtle bodies of the quantum model – the vital, mental, supramental and bliss bodies – lie within this realm.

In his interview with *The Optimist Magazine*, Russian physicist Dr. Yuri Kronn informs us that matter and electromagnetic energy occupy only 4% of the universe, and the subtle energy that cannot be seen or measured fills 96% of the universe. "We can't measure it. But we know it's there, because we can observe the effects of subtle energy on inanimate matter and living organisms" (Kamp, 2016, p. 42). Dr. Kronn was involved in experiments with Dr. Yan Xin, a qigong master and medical doctor who could repeatedly affect the half-life of a radioactive substance, americium-24, by projecting subtle energy or chi to it. Dr. Kronn tells us:

> It is important to note that neither electrical nor magnetic fields, no matter how strong, can influence the decay rate of radioactive elements. But Yan's chi does modify the characteristic behavior of matter. The only logical conclusion is that chi interacts with the particles that make protons and neutrons, quarks or the even tinier particles, sub quarks, that make quarks," says Kronn. "It means that chi or subtle energy belongs to and acts in the subatomic world. It also means that subtle energy is a fifth force next to the four fundamental forces known to science—electromagnetic, gravitational, strong and weak forces (Kamp, 2016, p. 43).

Harold Saxton Burr at Yale University researched the concept of energy fields and health in the 1930's. Burr discovered the existence of what he called L-fields (living fields). In his book, *The Blueprint for Immortality*, Burr described the importance of these L-fields in that all living objects are "molded and controlled by "electrodynamic fields" which are the "basic blueprints of all life on this planet" (Rosch, 2015, p. 94). Burr demonstrated that these L-Fields could be measured and postulated, "Since measurements of L-field voltages can reveal physical and mental conditions, doctors will be able to use them to diagnose illness before the usual symptoms develop and so will have a better chance of successful treatment." (Rosch, 2015, p. 595) Highly sensitive devises such as magnetoenchephalography and the Super Quantum Interface Device (SQUID) have verified that these L-Fields do reflect physical as well as emotional health (Rosch pg. 595).

Around this same time period, Alexander Gurwitsch, Ph.D. investigated the role of energy fields and biology while studying developmental biology. Gurwitsch's Morphogenetic Field Theory attributes the development of organisms to more than merely interactions between elements; rather development is the result of a field of forces that regulate the behavior of cells. These fields are coherent processes that guide embryonic development as well as the growth, development and regeneration of cell (Wijk, 2014, p. 88). In his famous "onion experiment", Gurwitsch was able to show that a form of radiation emanating from the tip of an onion root was able to stimulate mitosis (cell division) in an adjacent onion root. The results could not be explained by chemical or mechanical theories (Wijk, 2014, p. 89). Another prominent developmental biologist, Hans Driesch, discovered that this morphogenetic field remained even when portions of embryonic tissue were removed. It was proposed that this morphogenetic field was a property of the entire organism that helped to guide the development of cells and organs (Rubik, Muehsan, Hammerschlag, & Jain Ph.D., 2015). Gurwitsch's work was confirmed in the 1970's (Popp, Pressman, Konig and Fisher), and developed further to demonstrate that electromagnetic fields play a role in the regulation of information in living systems (Swanson, 2010, p. 471). In the quantum model of medicine, these morphogenetic fields are associated with the level of the vital body.

Free flow of energy, chi, within this level of the vital body is essential for health. The philosophy of Homeopathic Medicine is based on the precept that illness results from a disruption in the vital force of the organism. In his groundbreaking work, *The Organon of Medicine*, Dr. Samuel Hahnemann provides this perspective of health:
> In the healthy condition of man, the spiritual force, the dynamis that animates the material body, rules with unbounded sway and retains all parts of the organism in admirable, harmonious vital operation, as regards both sensation and function, so that our indwelling, reason-gifted mind can freely employ this living healthy instrument for the higher purposes of our existence (Hahnemann, 1982, aphorism 9).

Hahnemann postulated that the vital force animates the body and strives continually for balance or homeostasis. The force itself is not visible to the naked eye, yet its effects on the organism can be observed. A disturbance in the vital energies of the organism becomes evident, manifesting as symptoms on the physical and/or the subtle energy bodies. From a homeopathic perspective, all disease is an external manifestation of an internal physiological and energetic disorder unique to the individual.

In his seminal work, *Vibrational Medicine*, Richard Gerber, MD, describes this shift in viewing life from a mechanical to an energetic perspective.
> The Einsteinian paradigm as applied to vibrational medicine sees human beings as networks of complex energy fields that interface with

physical/cellular systems. Vibrational medicine attempts to interface with primary subtle energy fields that underlie and contribute to the functional expression of the physical body (Gerber, 1998, p. 39).
James Oschman provides a history of the research and use of energetic therapies in living organisms. Oschman's book, *Energy Medicine: The Scientific Basis,* covers extensive research providing a scientific basis as to why chemical communication no longer adequately explains the incalculable array of processes occurring in living organisms. He concludes that many processes even supersede our conventional notions of electromagnetic communication. "The mechanisms involved are various quantum processes including quantum coherence as described by Herbert Frölich, spin resonance as described by Mae Wan Ho and Emilio Del Giudice, biophotonic communication as described by Fritz Albert Popp" (Rosch, 2015, p. 454).

Discoveries are proving that frequency (energy) is the language of communication within the living organism. The work of Bruce Lipton in his book, *The Biology of Belief,* reinforces the findings of researchers mentioned above. Lipton calls for a revision in our current understanding that cells receive and process information purely on a chemical basis. Lipton states that, "Receptor antennas can also read vibrational energy fields such as light, sound, and radio frequencies. The antennas on these energy receptors vibrate like tuning forks. If an energy vibration in the environment resonates with a receptor's antenna, it will alter the protein's charge, causing the receptor to change (its) shape" (Lipton, 2005, p. 83). This was the work of Dr. Herbert Fröhlich who discovered that biomolecules emit and receive electromagnetic as well as vibrational energy. The receiving or sending of energy causes a change in shape, which induces a change in behavior. Fröhlich provided mathematical models to demonstrate the foundation for the work of Dr. Fritz-Albert Popp, who proposed that it is light (energy), in the form of biophotons that provides the mode of communication between molecules and cells (Swanson, 2010, p. *473).*

> When atoms or molecules create electromagnetic energy, they do so in small quantized packets called photons. It results from a change in the quantum state of the atom or molecule. A photon is a wave of electromagnetic energy. A specific frequency of a wave will have a precise amount of energy, as dictated by quantum physics. When such a wave encounters an electrical charge on a molecule, it exerts a force on it causing the charge to vibrate...transferring the energy to it. If its vibrational frequency is resonant, the molecule will absorb the energy from the photon, raising its energy and changing its shape. This can set off a chain reaction of other chemical activities (Swanson, 2010, p. 474).

It is known by the work of Fritz Popp that DNA is both a receiver and transmitter of biophotons, providing an explanation of DNA's control of molecules. This system of electromagnetism, electromechanical vibrations and the molecular response is collectively called the Bioelectromagnetic Field.

The Office of Alternative Medicine (OAM) at the US National Institutes of Health (NIH) now recognizes this network of complex energy fields as the Bioelectromagnetic Field or Biofield for short. The OAM defines the Biofield and the Subtle Energy Field as

> A mass-less field, not necessarily electromagnetic, that surrounds and permeates living bodies and affects the body...The Biofield, a complex organizing energy field engaged in the generation, maintenance, and regulation of biological

homeodynamics, is a useful concept that provides the rudiments of a scientific foundation for energy medicine and thereby advances the research and practice of it (Rubik, Muehsan, Hammerschlag, & Jain Ph.D., 2015).

In a paper titled *The Biofield Hypothesis*, Rubik further develops the concept of the Biofield as a concept for understanding energy medicine from a scientific basis. The Biofield theory, "offers a unifying hypothesis to explain the interaction of objects or fields with the organism, and is especially useful toward understanding the scientific basis of energy medicine, including acupuncture, biofield therapies, Bioelectromagnetic therapies, and homeopathy" (Rubik, 2002, p. 703). The OAM recognizes the existence of this complex of energy fields comprising both electromagnetic forces as well as forces outside those dictated by the laws of classical physics.

However, the Biofield Theory remains a hypothesis as controversy still subsist as to the existence of those subtle energy fields that lie outside the detectable realms of classical physics. The National Center for Complementary and Alternative Medicine (NCCAM) draws a distinction between those energies that are scientifically observable and verifiable ("Veritable Energy Medicine"), and those that are unverifiable, yet to be measured ("Putative Energy Medicine). This line continues to dismiss subtle energies as outside the realm of detection, therefore scientifically invalid, continuing to exclude their relevance to health and healing. As Oschman points out in his second edition of *Energy Medicine*,

> To refer to bio fields as 'physically undetectable' or 'putative' is inappropriate because they are in fact measurable...A discovery in quantum physics led to the development of instruments (SQUID) that can map the energy fields of the human body with unprecedented sensitivity and accuracy. For

example, there are devices that can pick up the field of the heart fifteen feet away from the body…SQUIDSs are now being used in medical research laboratories around the world to map the bio magnetic fields produced by physiological processes inside the human body" (Oschman, 2016, p. 116, 331).

4 BIOACOUSTIC FREQUENCIES AND SOUND THERAPY

The term "bioacoustics" is used to describe a cross-disciplinary science combining biology and acoustics. It concerns sounds produced by or affecting living organisms, especially as relating to communication. In the field of bioacoustics, scientists study the anatomy and neurophysiology involved in sound production. Most of this work relates to animals, and the relationship of response to sound cues in the environment, and the organs and neuronal networks involved in the process ("Bioacoustics," 2016). Sound therapy, is a type of vibrational medicine that uses the human voice as well as objects that resonate (Tibetan bowls, tuning forks, etc.) to stimulate healing.

Sound healing differs from music therapy in significant ways. Firstly, sound healing is an eclectic combination of practices derived from esoteric, contemplative and meditative, as well as spiritual practices, which use a range of hypothetical principles to explain or describe its processes, including those derived from Pythagorean theories, Hindu theology, and Christian religion ("Sound healing," November 2005, p. 1).

For his profound contributions to the field of sound therapy, we can examine the pioneering work of Dr. Alfred Tomatis. He discovered that listening is the first sense we develop in utero, and that a fetus hears and responds to sound pulses even before physical development of the ear ("Listening, Learning and Development Center in Calgary," 2016, p. 1). At four and a half months before birth, the ear is already listening. It was his deep conviction that sound and the act of listening, which starts in the womb, is essential for proper physical and psychological development, that, "listening is a high level ability that opens directly into consciousness....a dialectic is set up between consciousness and listening, by means of which the one is more active as the other grows" (Tomatis, 1991, p. 208). He draws a distinction between hearing and listening, the former being passive, the latter involving an act of will. "To listen is to want to hear and then apply oneself to do so…it is to pass from mere sensation to perception" (Tomatis, 1991, p. 206). The *Tomatis Method* and his patented Electronic Ear has contributed to a deeper understanding of communication, language and learning, bearing impact on the fields of education, psychology, audiology, speech and even childbirth (Tomatis, 1991). His book, *The Conscious Ear*, details the development of his life's work, which has helped address issues such as stuttering, autism, dyslexia, and motor control. Tomatis concludes that the function of the ear is to charge the nervous system, and since our body is the first thing to be affected by the sounds we utter, we transform our body as we speak (Tomatis, 1991, p. 81).

    Using sound as a healing modality has been prevalent in many cultures throughout history, and is still being used by many native cultures today. Pythagoras, Plato and Aristotle taught about the effects of sound and healing. The healing ceremonies of indigenous people incorporate sound, rhythm and music as an important part of the process. Recently, there has been a resurgence of interest in sound as a healing modality as it has been proven to be an effective form of alternative therapy in a variety of medical settings. A recent article published by the American Psychological Association summarizes a number of studies providing evidence of how music therapy improved the health outcomes in a variety of settings (Novotney, 2013, p. 1) The first study discussed was published in Pediatrics, 2013, which suggested that some sounds may soothe pre-term babies, improve the infants' sleeping and eating patterns, and decrease parents' levels of stress. Another study published in *Trends in Cognitive Sciences*, April 2013, states:

> The researchers found that listening to and playing music increase the body's production of the antibody immunoglobulin A and natural killer cells — the cells that attack invading viruses and boost the immune system's effectiveness. Music also reduces levels of the stress hormone cortisol.

Another study reported in the same article reviewed research in Parkinson's patients conducted at the Sun Life Financial Movement Disorders Research and Rehabilitation Centre at Wilfrid Laurier University, in Waterloo, Ontario. By using a novel form of frequency treatment known as *Vibroacoustic Therapy,* patients with Parkinson's disease showed improvements in symptoms such as less rigidity and better speed in walking with longer steps and reduced tremors (*NeuroRehabilitation*, December, 2009).

Recent innovations in healing with sound and frequency originate from a woman with a truly unique gift. Sharry Edwards was born with the unique ability to hear frequencies outside of the range of normal human hearing. With this ability, she is able to detect missing or dissonant sounds in a person's voice pattern and discovered that feeding back these missing sounds can lead to healing.

> Edwards has demonstrated that the human voice is a unique frequency representation of the body's structural and biochemical status, and that, through the use of voice spectral analysis techniques she developed, the body is capable of diagnosing and prescribing for itself" ("Top Health," p. 1).

The system known as "Vocal Profiling" uses sophisticated electronics to analyze an individual's voice pattern and determine which frequencies to feedback to the body for use in healing. This therapy is being used to assist in numerous issues including macular degeneration, multiple sclerosis, headaches, stress, and brain trauma. In Edwards' own words she explains:

> I can hear and duplicate the sounds/frequencies that people need to balance and become well. The sounds I hear turned out to be the morphogenic resonance (of plants) and described as a Signature Sound in ancient healing literature and an oto-acoustic emission by modern science (Edwards, 2001, p. 1).

Recent research the Institute of BioAcoustic Biology and Sound Health is exploring the hypothesis that, "ancient architecture and language contain math codes that support frequency-based cellular generation" (Edwards, p. 1)

Dr. Mitchell Gaynor, author of *The Healing Power of Sound* and board certified medical oncologist and the former director of medical oncology at the Weill Cornell Center for Complementary and Integrative Medicine actively uses sound in his healing practice. Gaynor started using quartz crystal and Tibetan singing bowls in his practice in the early 1990's. In a transcript of a recent interview with Bill Thompson, Dr. Gaynor, states the following:

> Sound can change immune function, "your interleukin-1 level, and index of your immune system, goes up between 12 and a half to 15 percent…about 20 minutes after listening to this meditative music, your immunoglobulin levels in your blood are significantly increased. There's no part of our body not affected. Even our heart rate and blood pressure are lowered with certain forms of music…it affects us on a sub-cellular level ("Delamora Sound & Evolution," p. 1).

Inspired by the work of Tomatis, musician, acupuncturist and bio-energetician, Fabien Maman has taken an innovative approach in researching the effects of sound healing. His book, *The Tao of Sound*, represents thirty-five years of research into the effects of sound on human cells, documented with a Kirlian camera. Maman's experiments focused on various acoustic instruments such as the gong, acoustical guitar, xylophone, and the human voice as he believed that only acoustics harmonics produce health

> Acoustic sound is alive. It resonates with the natural overtones or harmonies present in nature, not only on the physical level in human cells, but also in the subtle energy fields around the cell. Electric sound (anything from radio waves to electric guitars) has no overtone, and therefore, contains no real chi - the life-giving essence that nurtures the physical body or the electromagnetic field (Maman & Unsoeld, 2016, p. 11).

Maman proved that the cells' shape and subtle energy field change with different pitches and timbre of notes. The pictures in his book, *The Tao of Sound*, illustrate how the cell's subtle energy fields change color and transform into a mandala shape with vibrant colors of pinks and blues when the cell felt a 'vibratory affinity' with a certain note" (Unsoeld, 2005, p. 1). Since electronic instruments lose at least fifty percent of the overtones needed to nourish the subtle bodies, Maman uses only acoustic instruments in his work and on his recordings. Through his research, Maman was able to demonstrate that in healthy cells:

- The electromagnetic field is revitalized by certain acoustic sounds,
- This field changes shape and color depending on pitch of the note and timbre of the instrument,
- Each cell has a certain 'vibratory affinity' that when reached transforms the cell into a

mandala of colors – pink, magenta, and turquoise (Maman & Unsoeld, 2016, p. 84). In contrast, when it came to cancer cells, Maman found the following:

- Certain acoustic sounds can destabilize the cell leading to their explosion,
- They are inflexible and stuck in their structure,
- The chromatic scale, played in a systematic progression had the most dramatic impact, seemingly unable to support "a progressive accumulation of vibratory frequencies" (Maman & Unsoeld, 2016, p. 85).

Perhaps most profound, Maman documented that, *"The human voice produced the most dramatic results –* exploding cancer cells and energizing healthy ones; however, the rich overtones of the gong being played for 21 minutes also caused the cancer cells to disintegrate and ultimately explode" (italics added) ("Delamora Sound & Evolution," p. 1). Maman explains, "With the human voice, singing the chromatic scale, the HeLa (cancer) cells exploded more rapidly and predictably. This was because the human voice has an additional quality not found in a musical instrument: *consciousness"* (Maman & Unsoeld, 2016, p. 85)

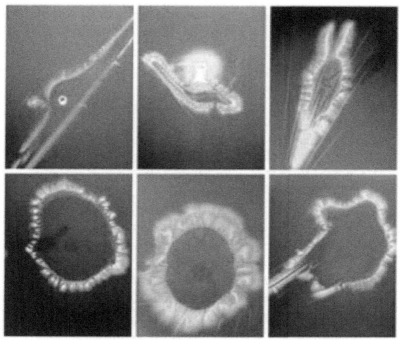

Figure 1 Kirlian Photograph of Acoustic Sounds on Healthy Human Cells, © Fabien Maman

Herbert Fröhlich has demonstrated that tissue and organs have collective frequencies that regulate cellular processes. When this frequency is altered, loss of coherence ensues that can lead to disease. As Oschman eloquently states, "While pathology may manifest as chemical imbalances, the underlying problem is electromagnetic (i.e. energetic). Hence providing the correct frequencies can often restore balance or 'healthy' vibration entraining the oscillations back to coherence (Oschman, 2002, p. 135). Dr. Leonard Horowitz and Dr. Joseph Puleo state that these healthy balances can be entrained by the original Solfeggio frequencies of the ancient Gregorian chants. The frequencies when sung in Latin were believed to impart spiritual blessings. "The combination of these sacred tones and the Latin intonation had the power to penetrate deep into the recesses of the subconscious mind and promote great healing and transformation (Mowry, p. 1).

The Solfeggio Frequencies

In the 1970's, Dr. Joseph Puleo, found six electro-magnetic sound frequencies that corresponded to the syllables from the hymn to St. John the Baptist:
"**Ut** queant laxis **Re**sonare fibris, **Mi**ra gestorum **Fa**muli tuorum, **Sol**ve polluti **La**bii reatum"
The Solfeggio frequencies are tuned to different scale than our modern day scale. This suggests an out of attunement with our modern music and an omission of critical tones and vibrations. The Solfeggio is tuned to the scale of ancient Egyptian and Greek instruments at 432 Hz. "This 432 Hz touches the full twelve scale octaval overtones of all music in creation, whereas Bach's 440 Hz only touches 8, leaving out an entire section of the complete musical resonance of the universe" ("The Cycle of Time Number 432," p. 1).

> *The American Federation of Musicians accepted the A440 as standard pitch in 1917. The U.S. government accepted it as its standard in 1920. It was not until 1939 that this pitch was accepted internationally and then standardized by the International Organization for Standardization in 1955 to serve as the audio frequency reference for the calibration of pianos, violins, and other musical instruments...A432 was often used by Classical composers and results in a tuning of the whole number frequencies that are connected to numbers used in the construction of a variety of ancient works and Sacred sites, such as the Great Pyramid of Egypt. The original Stradivarius violin was designed to be tuned to 432hz. The archaic*

Egyptian instruments that have been unearthed, so far, are largely tuned to 432hz. In ancient Greece (the school book original place for music) their instruments were predominantly tuned to 432hz. ("The Cycle of Time Number 432," p. 1)

Each of the Solfeggio frequencies corresponds to a note, color and chakra of the body.

Chakra	Solfeggio Frequency	Standard Scale	Meaning
Root	"UT" 396 Hz	261.63 Hz	Grounding, Turning Grief into Joy, Liberating Guilt & Fear
Sacral	"RE" 417 Hz	293.66 Hz	Undoing Situations and Facilitating Change
Solar Plexus	"MI" 528 Hz	329.63 Hz	Transformation and Miracles
Heart	"FA" 639 Hz	349.23 Hz	Connecting/ Relationships
Throat	"SOL" 41 Hz	392.00 Hz	Expression/ Solutions
Brow	"LA" 52 Hz	440.00 Hz	Awakening Intuition/ Spiritual Balance
Crown	"TI" 963 Hz	439.88 Hz	Communication with Divine, Higher Dimensions

Harmonics and Healing Resonance in Nature

Harmonics or overtones are only found in acoustic instruments, the human voice and nature itself. Again, Maman explains that the key to this resides in the nature of acoustic sound:
> X Acoustic sound offers space and time between each note through its overtones (harmonics). Overtones are like a natural wave that expands, we breathe in the space between the notes. It is in this space that real healing occurs…And in nature itself, overtones can be found in the wind in the trees or the call of a bird or the drops of water in a stream (Maman & Unsoeld, 2016, p. 91).

In a similar manner, Anthony Fiorenza has developed what he calls "Astrophysical-Bio-Harmonic Resonances" (Fiorenza, 2003-2016, p. 1). His background as a researcher, engineer and developer of diagnostic medical instruments, provided the basis for the creation of audio compositions based on the harmonics of nature and the signals of the planets in our solar system. Fiorenza believes that our health is influenced by these frequencies as they create the harmonic environment in which all life on earth evolves. "Our biological and neurological systems function in attunement to this astrophysical symphony. Each planetary harmonic signature resonates with its corresponding neurological aspect within us—our entire mental, emotional and physical composition (Fiorenza, 2003-2016, p. 1). His exploratory research in the 1980's revealed that the use of specific frequencies of color, sound, geometry and planetary harmonics produced positive healing responses on physical, emotional and mental levels.

His article, *Planetary Harmonics and Neurobiological Resonances,* details the mathematical process of converting audio tones to the corresponding color in the visible spectrum of light. The visible spectrum of color is forty times higher than the audio octave. Through his mathematical computations, he was able to convert the frequencies found in nature and the planets, into an audible range, creating audio compilations to assist in healing.

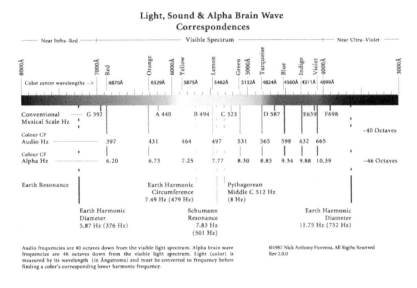

Figure 2 Frequency Correspondence Chart © Anthony Fiorenza

Numerous researchers are finding that attuning to these natural frequencies can be very difficult in our modern environment due to the electromagnetic fields (EMF) that disrupt these natural frequencies. Cell phones, microwaves and power grids are disruptive to the reception of these natural frequencies, ultimately resulting in poor health. A recent newsletter published by one of Dr. Kronn's staff members, Galinda Kalyruzhny, shows that the amount of research conducted regarding the effect of EMF's on living organisms has been sharply rising over the past twenty years. The article presents a number of facts concerning the disruptions these fields can create.

- The former Soviet Union described "microwave sickness" in military employees working with radio and radar equipment in the 1950's. Some of the symptoms reported were headaches, disturbances in sleep, concentration and memory, fatigue dizziness, irritability, burning skin and cardiac irregularities.
- Current research indicates that, "there is strong evidence that long-term exposure to certain Electromagnetic fields (EMFs) is a risk factor for illnesses such as certain cancers, memory performance, male infertility, and the developing electromagnetic hypersensitivity " (Kalyuzhny, Volume 4 Number 121, September 2016, p. 1).

This newsletter links to a study sponsored by the European Commission of Health and Consumer Protection, regarding newly identified risks and possible effects of EMF on human health. The Committee finds that while evidence for the effects of all the forms of EMF remains inconclusive, some forms produce deleterious effects. "The previous conclusion that Extremely Low Frequency (ELF) magnetic fields are possibly carcinogenic, chiefly based on childhood leukemia results, is still valid. There is no generally accepted mechanism to explain how ELF magnetic field exposure may cause leukemia" (Ahlbom, Bridges, & Mattson, 2007, p. 7). And further exploration into the effects of various living organisms concluded that more research is warranted.

The continued lack of good quality data in relevant species means that there are insufficient data to identify whether a single exposure standard is appropriate to protect all environmental species from EMF. Similarly the data are inadequate to judge whether the environmental standards should be the same or significantly different from those appropriate to protect human health. Research Recommendations: Important research needs were identified within all frequency bands (Ahlbom et al., 2007, p. 7).

The following table from the committee's report defines the types of various EMF's, and some of the sources of exposure (see below).

Type of EMF	Frequency Range	Sources of Exposure
Static Fields (SF)	0 Hz	VDU (video displays); MRI and other diagnostic / scientific instrumentation; Industrial electrolysis; Welding devices
Extremely Low Frequency Fields (ELF)	0-300 Hz	Power lines; Domestic distribution lines, Domestic appliances; Electric engines in cars, train and tramway; Welding devices
Intermediate Frequency Fields (IF)	300 HZ – 100 kHz	Anti theft devices in shops, hands free access control systems, card readers and metal detectors, MRI
Radio Frequency Fields (RF)	100 kHz – 300 GHz	Mobile telephones; Broadcasting and TV; Microwave oven; Radar, portable and stationary radio transceivers, personal mobile radio

Fiorenza provides an explanation as to why EMF's can be so disruptive to the health and regulation within living organisms.

> This is due to the quantum-biochemical fact that intercellular and genetic communication occurs via light (electrons and photons), which is easily disrupted and distorted by external man-made EMF fields...Man-made electromagnetic radiation can cause everything from brain cell DNA damage to sever alterations in health, mood, emotional stability and behavior... We are not intended to function at one specific frequency. Entraining ourselves with artificially generated frequencies for extended periods, whether 8 Hz or by the 50 and 60 Hz power fields and radio frequency pollution we live in, can be debilitating and is dangerous. It can create degeneration, disease, mental, emotional, physical disharmony and imbalance. Most importantly, it can keep us from receiving and integrating the cosmic intelligence provided by mother Earth in a harmonious way (Fiorenza, 2003-2016, p. 2).

One of these healing frequencies, the Schumann resonance, has been the subject of a wide variety of recent research for its connection to health. Schumann discovered that the ionosphere surrounding the earth is a huge cavity resonator, much like a violin. And of the frequencies that travel within this cavity the fundamental frequency is 7.8 Hertz. This is of considerable significance. "The main command center of the human brain, the hippocampus / hypothalamus, vibrates at the same frequency of 7.8 Hz; this area of the brain is important for attentiveness and concentration" ("Advanced Medical Systems / Institute of Biophysics Bioinformative Medicine - developed by Dr. Wolfgang Ludwig®," 2010, p. 15-16).

These various resonant earth frequencies have an effect on brain waves. Studies have found that the EEG of the human brain fluctuates in concert with the natural fluctuations of the Schumann resonance throughout the course of a day (Rosch, 2015, p. 414). Due to the variation is the size of the ionosphere at different points in the earth this resonance varies. The other frequency peaks of the Schumann resonance – 14, 20, 26, 33 39, and 45 Hz - align closely with various brain wave states: alpha (8 – 12 Hz), beta (12-30 Hz), and gamma (30 – 100 Hz). Research indicates that these fluctuating signals have an effect on the brain waves altering neuro-hormonal responses (Rosch, 2015, p. 414). As discussed previously, electronic generation of frequencies do not produce natural harmonics or overtones found in nature, and could be more harmful than healing when used for therapeutic purposes. Again, Fiorenza explains:

"Because of the entraining capacity of single electronically generated frequencies, if they are used for sustained periods, they can trigger and hold a person in any number of psycho-emotional states.... This type of entrainment already occurs due to the 50 and 60 Hertz electromagnetic fields people live in daily and the electronic devices they live with—including TV's and computers. For this reason, and when using frequencies for healing purposes, specific frequencies should be used in sequences or progressions designed to bring a person completely through a healing crisis rather than simply trigger the condition, or worse yet, sustain it" (Fiorenza, 2003-2016, p. 1).

Rife Therapy

Rife Therapy is a form of frequency therapy that was embraced by many physicians in the 1930's until it was driven underground by the pharmaceutical interests and the American Medical Association. Royal Raymond Rife designed and built many instruments for medical research including his unique Universal Microscope that allowed microbes to be viewed in their living state. With this ability he was able to study pathogens and made a groundbreaking discovery. When a virus or bacterium was exposed to a particular frequency, the pathogen would grow weak or break apart. *The Rife Handbook* states that,

> The microbe's frequency (the number of cycles per second at which it vibrated) was also known as its Mortal Oscillatory Rate (MOR). An analogy explaining how Rife's ray tube worked was the cliché of the soprano, who shatters a glass with her pure, focused tone. If enough power were applied, the resonant frequency killed the microbe or debilitated it enough so that the body's own immune cells could then dispose of it (Sylver, 2011, p. 674).

Since a person or animal has a much more complex structure than the pathogen, the MOR frequency will only harm the microbe. In his paper *Healing with Electromedicine and Sound Therapies*; Nenah Sylver details the science, research and history behind Rife and other frequency technologies. Sylver says that some tones within the range of human hearing can be substituted therapeutically for various electromagnetic frequencies. "Since sound and EM radiation are mathematically related, theoretically, all electromagnetic waves can be translated into audible sound, and the two modalities might be interchangeable for healing purposes (Sylver, 2011, p. 684). Sylver summarizes frequency and healing as follows:

> All biological functions correspond to electromagnetic phenomena. The electromagnetic energies that exist in living tissue are extremely potent. When you target a living cell with the precise frequency that it needs, it will respond favorably, and health can be restored in an amazingly short period of time…Every frequency in the EM spectrum has a corresponding sound, even if we cannot hear it. Thus, audible sound has an intricate relationship to EM frequencies and can also be utilized for healing (Sylver, 2011, p. 686).

5 TOOLS FOR MONITORING THE HUMAN BIOFIELD

As Albert Szent-Györgyi suggested, "some fundamental fact, if not a whole dimension, is missing from our biological thinking". It is logical then that we must devise new methods that help observe and study this new dimension. From this, we can expand our current model to include the subtle energy fields in our system of healing. Meeting these needs to better the degree that it can be applied to therapeutic practices calls for new tool and techniques.

✗ Heart Rate Variability

Heart Rate Variability (HRV) is quickly gaining recognition as an indicator of health. In contrast to the belief that a steady heart rate is ideal, it is now known that variability is normal and desired, and the loss of HRV is a strong indicator of disease and future health problems (McCraty, 2015, p. 35). Several companies have developed diagnostic tools for computerized, qualitative assessment of HRV and the functional level of the autonomic nervous system and HRV based on scientific, medical research conducted in Russia, Germany, France and the United States over the last 30 years. The HeartMath Research Center and Nerve Express HRV Testing System are two such systems.

Heart rhythms indicate how stressors (physically, mentally and emotionally) are affecting the nervous system. Coherent heart rhythms differ from simple relaxation; these rhythms place the individual in a state of improved functioning on physical, mental and emotional levels. Years of research conducted by the HeartMath Institute reveals that the variability in the heart's rhythms correlates with the function of the autonomic nervous system thus affecting all other systems in the body. Their research helped establish that the heart is more than a mechanical pump.

> The heart is, in fact, a highly complex information processing center with its own functional 'brain', commonly called the heart-brain that communicates with and influences the cranial brain via the nervous system, hormonal system, and other pathways. The influences affect brain function and most of the body's major organs and play an important role in mental and emotional experience and the quality of our lives. Healthy optimal function is a result of continuous, dynamic bi-directional interactions among multiple neural, hormonal and mechanical control systems at both local and central levels ("emWave Library," 2017).

Investigative research conducted by the HeartMath Institute concludes that,

> An optimal level of HRV within an organism reflects healthy function and inherent self-regulatory capacity, adaptability, and resilience. While too much instability, such as arrhythmias and chaos, is detrimental to efficient physiological functioning and energy utilization, too little variation indicates age-related system depletion, chronic stress, pathology or inadequate functioning in various levels of self regulatory control system (McCraty, 2015, p. 13).

A study published in the *American Journal of Epidemiology* finds that reduced heart rate variability is associated with many diseases such as cardiovascular, diabetes, and mortality in chronic disease as well as anxiety and depression (Dekker et al., 1997, p. 899). Another study finds that reduced overall HRV and loss of parasympathetic/sympathetic tone in youth with Type I Diabetes, contributes to cardiac autonomic neuropathy (Jaiswal et al., 2013, p. 157). The well-known 1994 Framingham Heart Study revealed that HRV is a predictive indicator of cardiovascular disease even beyond those found by traditional evaluation, and that increased HRV was the only factor found in healthy individuals. (Tsuji et al., 1996, p. 2850) In addition, the risks for cardiovascular disease (CVD) as determined by the Framingham Study found a correlation with HRV and CVD and also indicated that HRV may be of use as a non-invasive test for initial screening of CVD (Jelinek, Imam, A-Aubaidy, & Khandoker, 2013, p. 186). Finally, in Chronic Kidney Disease (CKD), multiple risk factors for renal and cardiovascular disease were found to be associated with lower HRV (Drawz et al., 2013, p. 517).

Substantial research conducted by the Institute of HeartMath for the past twenty-five years documents how techniques and therapies that assist in developing and increasing HRV correlate to improvement in a wide variety of health issues. Their research substantiates that the heart communicates on a variety of levels – electrically through the nervous system, biochemically through hormones and neurotransmitters, biophysically through pressure waves and energetically through electromagnetic field interactions (McCraty, 2015, p. 3). These levels of communication parallel the levels of the subtle energy bodies of the quantum model. The heart's electromagnetic field is the strongest, most powerful field produced by the body. The heart's electrical field is 60 times greater in amplitude of that of the brain. It is also 100 times greater than the magnetic field produced by the brain and can be detected 3 feet from the body with SQUID-based magnetometers (McCraty, 2015, p. 36).

Autonomic Nervous System Coherence

The term coherence refers to the order or harmony within a system. In physics, coherence means the synchronization or coupling between different oscillating fields. These coupled fields then become entrained to vibrate at the same frequency. Innovative research proves that coherent energy systems are fundamental to good health and precede chemical communication within living organisms. In her book *The Rainbow and the Worm*, Mae-Wan Ho, PhD argues that the specificity and rapidity with which intercommunication takes place in living systems can only be explained through the quantum coherence of energy systems (Ho, 2008, p. 285). Ho explains that this quantum coherent state, "in which every part of the body is intercommunicating and therefore functioning in the most efficient and coordinated way, " allows for reduced expenditure of energy and improved biomarkers for health. "Life", she states, "is a process of being an organizing whole" (Ho, 2008, p. 176).

The term physiological coherence is used to denote a condition of stability and degree of order in the rhythmic activity of living systems. This coherence signifies a system whose optimal and efficient functioning positively affects the ease and flow of life's processes (Rosch, 2015, p. 128). The Institute of Heart Math expands this definition to *psychophysiological* coherence, which include both physiological and psychological functioning, where the nervous system, cardiovascular, hormonal and immune systems are working at peak efficiency. This state of coherence is characterized by high heart rhythm, coherence of the autonomic nervous system with increased parasympathetic activity and decreased sympathetic activity. This coherence entrains and synchronizes physiological systems with harmonious functioning of the nervous, hormonal and immune systems (McCraty, 2015, p. 28). "Numerous studies have shown that heart coherence is an optimal physiological state associated with increased cognitive function, self-regulatory capacity, emotional stability and resilience" (McCraty, 2015, p. 28).

A hyperactive sympathetic system coupled with a hypoactive parasympathetic system is associated with various pathological conditions placing increased energy demands on the system accelerating aging and disease. Some of the pathologies associated with autonomic system imbalances include: depression, hypoglycemia, sleep disorder, irritable bowel, fibromyalgia, hypertension, premenstrual symptom, anxiety, migraines, and coronary artery disease (McCraty, 2015, p. 22). A study published in *The International Journal of Cardiology*, reviews the evidence linking reduced autonomic system coherence and HRV to the development of risk factors for disease. The authors suggest that autonomic imbalance may be a "final common pathway to increased morbidity and mortality from a host of conditions and diseases" (Thayer, Yamamoto, & Brosschot, 2010, p. 121). When the body is in a state of high coherence, "increased synchronization occurs between the sympathetic and parasympathetic branches of the autonomic nervous systems...benefitting both physiological and psychological functioning". As a result, improvements are seen in humoral immunity and increased DHEA/cortisol ratio (Rosch, 2015, p. 129).

Stressful "negative" attitudes and emotions, like frustration and anxiety cause chaotic heart rhythms – leading to increased cortisol level and disruptive sleep rhythm.

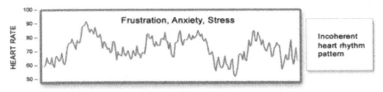

"Positive" attitudes and emotions, like appreciation, create smooth, coherent heart rhythms – leading to more restful and revitalizing sleep.

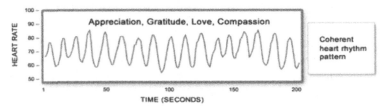

Figure 3. Incoherent vs. Coherent Heart Rhythm
© 2009 Institute of HeartMath

Research published in *Psychosomatic Medicine* concluded autonomic nervous system imbalance is a common factor contributing to obesity, diabetes, and heart disease, and that imbalance in autonomic function is a common underlying factor, as well as shown to be a risk factor and predictive of the development of metabolic syndrome (Wuslin, Horn, Perry, Massaro, & D'Angostino, 2015, p. 474). The authors suggest that since autonomic imbalance can be measured and responds to various different treatments, this marker has potential for indicating the efficacy of preventative therapies.

Further research illustrates that utilization of the self-regulation techniques patented by HeartMath (Quick Coherence and Heart Lock-In) creates positive effects on stress responses and various physiological systems. A study showed that the techniques used over a thirty-day period produced changes in biomarkers that indicate improved health, showing significant changes in DHEA

(100% increase) and cortisol levels (23% decrease). These changes correlated with emotional improvements in reduced stress and anxiety, and improved feelings of caring and vigor (McCraty, 2015, p. 53). "The implications are that relatively inexpensive interventions may dramatically and positively impact individuals' health and well-being" (McCraty, Barrios-Choplin, Rozman, Atkinson, & Watkins, 1998, p. 151). A study of hypertension in a risk – reduction program in the workplace achieved significant changes in systolic (10.6 mm Hg) and diastolic (6.3 mm Hg) blood pressure readings in comparison to a control group (3.7 mm Hg and 3.9 mm Hg respectively). Some of the participants were able to lower their BP medicine intake. Of note also was that the participants, "experienced significant reductions in stress and depression, concurrent with improvements in work performance-related parameters" (McCraty, 2015, p. 54). Another study showing significant improvement in physiological markers involved a risk reduction program involving 88 California police officers. The program used HeartMath's regulation techniques and HRV feedback. The study concludes: "Physiological changes in the experimental group included significant reductions in total cholesterol, LDL cholesterol levels, the total cholesterol /HDL ratio, fasting glucose levels, mean heart rate, mean arterial pressure, and both systolic and diastolic blood pressure" (McCraty, 2015, p. 55). The physiological improvements were accompanied by psychological improvements in decreased distress, anger, fatigue, hostility, and impatience while having improvements in gratitude and a positive outlook (McCraty, 2015, p. 56). A comprehensive overview of additional studies can be found in *Science of the Heart: Exploring the Role of Heart in Human Performance*, by Rollin McCraty and the HeartMath Institute. In addition to the above, this work covers research that documents how techniques that improve HRV and autonomic coherence positively improve physiological issues, such as asthma, congestive heart failure, hypertension, and chronic pain, in addition to psychological issues of cognitive function and memory, attention deficit hyperactivity disorder, post traumatic stress disorder, and overall mental health. The Institute has even conducted studies to illustrate how improvements in autonomic coherence and HRV can increase or augment development of intuition.

Ervin Laszlo argues that coherence in living organisms goes beyond biochemical parameters and is suggestive of quantum coherence.
> The living organism is extraordinarily coherent: All parts are multidimensionally, dynamically and almost instantly correlated with other parts. What happens to one cell or organ also happens in some way to all other cells and organs – a correlation that recalls (and in fact suggests) the kind of 'entanglement' that characterizes the behavior of quanta in the micro domain. The organism is also coherent with the world around it: What happens in the external milieu is reflected in some way in its internal milieu (Laszlo, 2077, p. 44).

Acupuncture and Electro Dermal Analysis

Archeological records indicate the use of acupuncture technique as far back as 1600 BC. Several texts such as *Nei Ching* (2600 BC), the *Canon of Medicine* (475 BC) and the *Analytical Dictionary of Characters* (206 BC) describe the meridian channels, treatments, counter-indications and pathological issues. The vital energy, or chi, is distributed via the meridian networks. This chi combines with the breath and circulates through all the systems of the body in pathways called meridians, and these meridians work in conjunction with each other to control bodily processes. Each meridian has its own direction of flow, and the intensity of that flow can be measured by electro diagnosis.

The introduction of acupuncture to the West centered on its use for pain relief and surgery. This meridian network is greater than the conventional understanding as a gateway to reduce pain. Since the meridians lack anatomical structure in the physical body, it has been difficult for conventional medicine to comprehend their existence and function. Through the model of Quantum Medicine, meridians are viewed as quantum entities. They represent a layer of consciousness in the subtle bodies (the vital body) providing a wealth of information to practitioners as to the health of the body.

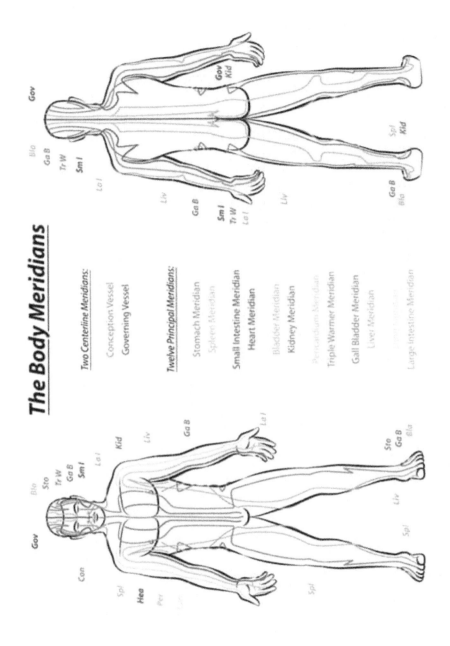

Figure 4. Meridians (Source www.sott.net/article/316751)

The acupuncture meridians comprise an organizing network for distribution, and utilization of information necessary for maintaining homeostasis. The SQUID provided a means for verification of acupuncture channels. Analogous to the body's internet, these meridians provide a system of instantaneous communication to all the various components of the body. Again, from Gerber, "The meridians distribute the subtle magnetic energies of chi which provide sustenance and organization for the physical-cellular structure of each organ system" (Gerber, 1998, p. 177). Free flow of energy through the meridians is essential to vibrant health. Impedance in that meridian indicates distortion of coherent communication that can manifest as a physical, emotional or mental disturbance. The ability to communicate instantaneously both locally and globally implies quantum coherence in the meridian network.

The next section contains a summary of the twelve acupuncture meridians their partners and associations, as well as the manifestations that result from balance and imbalance. Entire books have been written on this subject so this provides only a brief summary to introduce the breadth and depth of information that is available through this system. For more complete information, consult *The Web That Has No Weaver: Understanding Chinese Medicine*, by Ted Kaptchuk, or *Between Heaven and Earth: A Guide to Chinese Medicine,* by Beinfield and Korngold. As in convention, capital letters denote the meridian system, i.e. KIDNEY, to differentiate from the organ, i.e. kidney.

The Twelve Acupuncture Meridians

LIVER

The LIVER meridian corresponds with the spring and the Yin aspect of the element of Wood. It is considered the "General of the Army", with plans and visions for the future.

LIVER is associated with the Navel chakra, organs of liver, spleen, pancreas and gallbladder, the color yellow, and the note F#.

GALLBLADDER

The GALLBLADDER meridian is the Yang aspect of the element of Wood, and also spring. A balanced GALLBLADDER is the ground for "Courage & Decision"; it carries out the orders of the General (LIVER). GALLBLADDER is partner with LIVER, and corresponds to the note E.

LUNG

The LUNG meridian is the Yin aspect of the element of Metal and corresponds with autumn. The ability to "Embrace the Moment", to understand the ephemeral nature of life, defines a balanced LUNG meridian. LUNG associated with the Throat chakra, (and thyroid), the color blue, and the note G.

LARGE INTESTINE

LARGE INTESTINE is the Yang aspect of the element Metal and corresponds to autumn. This meridian "Moves the Turbid" and rules elimination, and is connected with the thyroid. LARGE INTESTINE is partner with LUNG; is associated with the sacral chakra (and the thyroid), and corresponds to the color orange and the note G#.

SPLEEN (PANCREAS)

SPLEEN represents the Yin aspect of the element of Earth and also corresponds to Late Summer. In Traditional Chinese Medicine, the spleen and pancreas are considered jointly in this meridian. SPLEEN is the meridian of "Transformation & Transportation" ruling digestion and absorption. SPLEEN is associated with the Navel chakra, the spleen, pancreas, liver and gallbladder, the color yellow and the note A#.

STOMACH

The STOMACH meridian is the Yang aspect of the element of Earth and corresponds to the season of Late Summer. It "Receives and Ripens" sending the pure to the SPLEEN. STOMACH is partner with SPLEEN; and corresponds to the note A.

HEART

The HEART is one of the Yin aspects of the element of Fire corresponding with summer. The HEART "Stores the Spirit", and allows our ability for connection and compassion with all of life. It nourishes the blood and shines the light of love on our perceptions. HEART is associated with the Heart chakra, the thymus, heart and lungs, the color green, and the note B.

SMALL INTESTINE

The SMALL INTESTINE is one of the Yang aspects of the element of Fire corresponding to summer. SMALL INTESTINE is the meridian that "Separates Pure from Impure". It is associated with the ability to separate thoughts and beliefs, truths and trusting in one's own judgment. SMALL INTESTINE is associated with the Navel chakra, yellow, and the note C.

PERICARDIUM (CIRCULATION)

PERICARDIUM is also a Yin aspect of the Fire element that corresponds to summer. It is considered the "Heart Protector", protecting the heart from over stimulation and shock. PERICARDIUM is associated with the Heart Chakra, the color green, and the note D#.

TRIPLE WARMER (TRIPLE HEATER)

TRIPLE WARMER is the other Yang aspect of the Fire meridian and corresponds to summer. The Endocrine system is represented through the TRIPLE WARMER. It directs the relationship between organs that regulate water, mediating between Water and Fire. TRIPLE WARMER is partner with PERICARDIUM; it corresponds with the note E.

KIDNEY

KIDNEY is the Yin aspect of the Water element and corresponds to winter. KIDNEY "Stores the Will"; it is the seat of the Life-essence, the pilot light of the body and the root of Water (Yin) and Fire (Yang). A balanced KIDNEY is the "Seat of Wisdom", and the ability to process the cycles of the birth, maturation and death, beginnings and endings. The right Kidney is associated with the Root chakra (as are the Adrenal glands), the color red, and the note D. The left Kidney is associated with the Sacral Chakra (as are the prostate, uterus, testes and ovaries), the color yellow and the note D.

BLADDER

The BLADDER meridian is the Yang aspect of the element of Water and corresponds to winter. This meridian receives and excretes urine, stores and eliminates waste. BLADDER is partner with KIDNEY, is associated with the Root Chakra, the color red and to the note C#.

In his second book on subtle energies, *Life Force, the Scientific Basis*, Claude Swanson delves into research on the acupuncture meridians. He describes the meridian system as,

> A network that ...serves as a communication system, linking all cells and organs in all parts of the body, providing the blueprint of growth which directs cell specialization and organ development and functioning...The meridian system also transports DNA, RNA and mitochondrial material, which may provide undifferentiated stem cells to help with tissue repair (Swanson, 2010, p. 140).

Swanson provides a summary of the work conducted by Korean scientist Kim Bonghan in the 1960s proving the existence of a duct system that follows the meridian channels. Also known as the Bonghan ducts, their existence was verified by injecting a radioactive tracer into the ducts and following it through the acupuncture system. These ducts were filled with a fluid which when analyzed were found to contain high quantities of DNA and RNA. The experiments of Dr. Kwang-Sup Soh in 2004 propose a model for how the bioenergy flows through the meridian network. Dr. Soh proposes that the DNA in the meridian channels absorb and re-emit biophotons (quantum packets of energy) which travel the network and act as boosting signals "enabling the signals to travel great distances throughout the body without losing strength or phase coherence" (Swanson, 2010, p. 143). This supports the seminal research of Dr. Fritz Popp whose work demonstrates that biophotons play a key role in the regulation, development and differentiation of cells. The biophoton field (i.e. energy, quantum energy) precedes and directs chemical and physical processes.

After developing bladder cancer in the 1940's, German medical doctor Reinhold Voll successfully sought answers for his own healing in traditional Chinese medicine and acupuncture. After this, he spent 20 years researching meridians and Chinese medicine (Grigorova, 2012, p. 37). With the assistance of Fritz Werner, an electrical engineer, Dr. Voll devised a system to study acupuncture pathways and the associated electrical conductance on the skin corresponding with traditional acupuncture points. Dr. Voll developed a method that combined the fundamentals of acupuncture with modern electronics for diagnostic procedures and assessing therapy (Leonhardt, 1980, p. 13). Originally called Electroacupuncture According to Voll (EAV), it is now more commonly known as Electro Dermal Analysis (EDA) to reflect its ability to provide an analysis.

Other groups of researchers refer to the testing as ElectroDermal Screening or Meridian Stress Analysis. Dr. Voll described the relationship between acupuncture points and their organ, finding new points and channels in the process. Additionally, Voll found correlations between conductance readings and certain pathological issues in tissues and organs. Along the lines of the work by Dr. Burr, Voll found that early disturbances in organ function could be noted through measureable energetic disturbances in the energy systems long before clinical symptoms appear. (Leonhardt, 1980, p. 15) Since the meridians conduct signals through biophoton communication of the DNA, when energy through a meridian is impeded, the signals will not arrive at strength sufficient to drive molecular processes and illness will result (Swanson, 2010, p. 153).

Extensive research by Dr. Voll and those who followed established the value of this form of testing for pre-diagnostic screening. EDA testing provides the ability to record progress over time providing objective proof of the efficacy of therapy – conventional or energetic. However, "Dr. Voll did not aim to replace traditional methods of diagnosis and therapy, but aimed to compliment methods in clinical medicine" (Leonhardt, 1980, p. 41). He felt strongly that the practice of EAV should be accompanied by knowledge of anatomy and clinical medicine, as well as pharmacology (allopathic and homeopathic) and Chinese acupuncture.

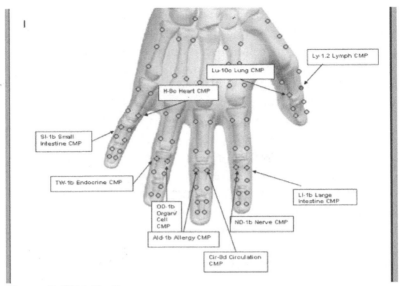

Figure 5. EDA Testing

The practice of Electro Dermal Analysis has been the subject of controversy regarding its accuracy or relevance to the analysis of conditions based on conventional diagnosis. These concerns are unwarranted; it has been proven that proper training develops the sensitivity to produce consistent, reproducible results regardless of the practitioner (Eanes, 2004). As regards to relevancy of medical conditions, numerous studies have been conducted that do show strong correlations with standard conventional analysis, including a landmark study published in 2003, which demonstrated a 99% correlation between the EDA measured abnormalities and patients with Chronic Inflammatory Demyelinating Polyneuropathy disease (Ericcson, Pittaway, & Lai, 2003, p. 1) Additional research by Drs. Tsuei and Lam, Voll, and Madill revealed correlations in EDA testing and diabetes mellitus, as well as inflammation, gastrointestinal issues and chronic degenerative diseases (Pittaway, 2002, p. 77 - 80). The article, *Bio-Energetic Medicine: The Past, Present and*

Future of the Electrodermal Screening System, states that Dr. Tsuei and colleagues completed over twenty studies using EDA. In the first study she states: "Conditions seen included peptic ulcers, appendicitis, chronic chorea, and cancer of the colon, breast and uterus. In every case, readings taken with EDA matched standard diagnostic tests" (Tsuei, 1996, p. 5). Dr. Tsuei provides a theoretical basis for EDA.

> The (EDA) is based on electromagnetic physics and quantum mechanics and this is well documented. Bio-energy, bio-information and harmonic resonance represent the biophysical foundation of its use. All living creatures generate energy containing biological information that flows in specific tracks throughout the organism. The cell mass in a given organ creates informational energy when the organ functions, giving rise to resonance. There is therefore a direct relationship between quality of organ function and the energy generated (Tsuei, 1996, p. 3).

Since inflammatory processes begin with increased energy production, this will register as an elevation in conductance through the meridian. This inflammatory process results in an increase in the concentration of ions, which correspond to the elevation in electrical conductance.

> This can be found even in those cases where the functions of the organ are still normal according to clinical and laboratory tests…Since the minute chemical reactions inside the cell represent displacements of energy, these shiftings can be seized and registered by electroacupuncture, long before the beginning of acute illness (Leonhardt, 1980, p. 21).

Low energy flow through the meridian substantiates Avicenna's philosophy stated earlier that, "pathology appears relatively late in the process, after the tissues have lost their energetic and metabolic means of responding (or reacting) to the disease." A decrease in electrical conductance indicates a degenerative condition or impedance of energy. This results in an accumulation of free radicals and a decrease in oxygen levels leading to a change in chemistry and eventually, changes in cellular manifestation. Leonhardt concludes that,

> EAV can be used for exact checking of success or failure of a therapy indicating the progress of healing or worsening of a pathological process…By the EAV-diagnosis, a sector of clinical medicine is covered which has been disregarded until now – the energy household (Leonhardt, 1980, p. 21).

EAV allows for us to fill the gap pronounced by Szent-Györgyi that, "Some fundamental fact, if not a whole dimension, is missing from our biological thinking."

It is important to note that EAV is not directly measuring the energy in the meridians of the body. Since this type of energy lies outside of the four primary forces of classical physics, direct measurement is not possible. However, "there is a bio-physiological phenomenon that occurs when you run electricity through the acupuncture points. The electrical flow (conductance) gives us an indication of the energetic health status of the meridian that we are testing" (Eanes, 2004, p. 2). Dr.. Voll discovered that regardless of who is being tested, each meridian has a Universal Baseline reading, which establishes EAV as a valuable testing procedure. The following provides a more detailed explanation.

> Regardless of who is tested, no matter what their age, weight, sex, nationality or race, a reading of 50 with no change over time (no indicator drop), is an indication of an energetically healthy meridian. Readings that are significantly above 50 (65 plus) indicate inflammation, and this is due to the fact that when tissue becomes inflamed, the

concentration of body fluids increases and therefore the conductance will increase accordingly. When a reading is significantly lower than 50 (below 30) then it is believed that this meridian is low energy or possibly degenerative. When a reading steadily drops in value from the high point down, this is known as an "Indicator Drop" (ID), and it can point to a weakness or disturbance in the meridian (Eanes, 2004, p. 2).

Indicator drops are an important marker in testing as they indicate an imbalance and can be used to determine the cause of the impedance or imbalance in the meridian. Additionally, the indicator drops are utilized to pretest the efficacy of remedies such as homeopathics, herbs and nutraceuticals.

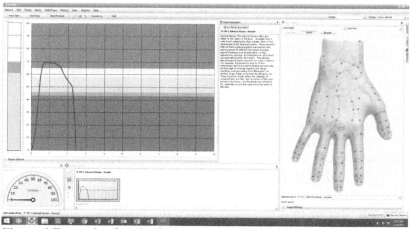

Figure 6 Example of an Indicator Drop Using EAV

Readings of test subjects will provide essentially the same results for any well-trained, experienced practitioners. This establishes EAV as a valid health screening modality because the test readings are reproducible (Eanes, 2004, p. 2). Since Voll, numerous studies have been conducted using EAV generating information from an expanded perspective on health. The *American Journal of Acupuncture* has published articles regarding its valid, scientific basis for a "true and legitimate preventative medicine" (Madill, 1979). The same journal published additional articles regarding the advantages in utilizing EAV as a testing method to assist in: hypoglycemia, stress and psychosomatic illness (Madill, 1980), to pre-test the efficacy of various medicines for different diseases (Voll, 1980), and to demonstrate the effectiveness for determining the correct dosage of allopathic or homeopathic medicines to treat diabetes mellitus, (F., Tsuei, & Zhao, 1990). Recently, a practitioner in Africa, Nadejda Grigorova published her extensive work of 11 years exploring EAV, homeopathy, quantum physics and the role of underlying viral, bacterial and fungal pathogens in diseases. A comprehensive list of published scientific studies in EAV can be found in the Electro Dermal Analysis Student Handbook from the Institute of Natural Health Sciences (Pittaway, 2002).

EAV empowers both quantum practitioner and the client by providing a system to locate the obstacles to healing within the subtle energy fields. In *Vibrational Medicine*, Gerber emphasizes the importance of this testing.

The ability to measure electromagnetic disturbances in the meridian system and find imbalances in the flow of chi allows one to detect ongoing cellular pathology in a particular area of the body as well as predict future organic dysfunction.... One is able to tap into the specialized internal bioenergy circuits, which connect the etheric, and physical energy fields...Electroacupuncture technologies may allow us to actually measure subtle energy imbalances, which are precursors to illness. In addition, these same technologies can reveal illness in the physical body, which is still too subtle to be measured by conventional laboratory tests (Gerber, 1998, p. 204 -

205).

Figure 7 Electro Dermal Analysis Testing

6 THE RESEARCH PROJECT

Measuring the Effects of Targeted Bioacoustic Frequencies

Objective
The purpose of this study is to determine if beneficial effects of energy medicine in the form of specific targeted bioacoustic frequencies (i.e. vibrational medicine) can be measured objectively using subtle energy biomarkers.

Background
One of the main difficulties with accepting the viability of energy medicine is that we are continually challenged to prove its beneficial effects. It is said that results of energy therapies are subjective, and without objective measurement fall outside the realm of science. With advanced technology we are now able to detect and observe the presence of the subtle energies that have been previously undetectable by conventional methods. This study proposes that the beneficial effects of energy medicine in the form of specific, targeted bioacoustic frequencies can be observed through objective measurements of the biomarkers of autonomic nervous system coherence, heart rate variability and meridian analysis. Research proves that improvement in any of these variables positively impacts a wide variety of parameters consistent with positive health.

Materials and Methods
The purpose of the study was three fold: first was to validate the proposed theory that the healing effects of energy medicine could have an objectively measured effect

on the energy systems as well as the physical body of the client. Second, to ensure that the results would be measureable and quantifiable in terms of improvements in health. Third, to determine if the independent variable, the compilation of specific, targeted bioacoustic frequencies (a therapeutic sound modality trademarked as Sayonic Therapy), could be used as an effective healing modality as a stand-alone therapy or to augment other forms of quantum medicine. A clinical analysis was designed to explore these goals. Tests for HRV and Coherence were conducted using HeartMath's emWave Pro Plus Coherence Training System, and the EAV tests were done with the Electro Acupuncture According to Dr. Voll/Electro Dermal Analysis using the Avatar Testing System.

Sayonic Therapy is a recorded compilation of specific targeted frequencies that resonate with homeostasis based on the research of Royal Rife and Wolfgang Ludwig, and the sounds, musical tones and words which have been reputed to be of value in healing or connected to spiritual states from a variety of cultures throughout history. The goal of Sayonic Therapy, an archaic term meaning "the language of frequency", is to utilize bioacoustic frequencies to assist the healing process. That is, to communicate through harmonic resonance the vibrational patterns found in nature to place the body in an optimal state for healing.

Prior to the development of the final compilation, preliminary testing of numerous sounds, vocal and instrumental, were conducted on volunteer subjects. Subjects ranged in age from 18 – 65 years of age. None of the test subjects were familiar with the testing equipment used or any of the techniques developed by HeartMath to assist with achieving states of high coherence. Informed consent was obtained from the participants. To make all frequencies audible, the frequencies that fall outside the range of human hearing were stepped up or down to the range of human hearing using the mathematical theories of music and harmonic resonance. In developing this therapy, the frequency patterns were produced using the human voice for two reasons: the ear is intricately connected to the sound of the voice from the beginning of development in utero, and the human voice produces more natural harmonics than any other instrument. Initial testing involved the following:

- Tibetan singing bowls,
- Crystal bowls,
- Chimes and finger symbols,
- Tibetan throat singing,
- Tuning forks
- Rain stick
- Wooden Flute
- Pythagorean tone generator
- Solfeggio tones,
- Ancient Scales,
- Frequencies of colors,
- Portal Tones,
- Sounds of nature (wind, water)
- Sounds from our solar system (recorded by NASA)
- Harmonics of the Schumann resonance
- Mantras of sacred words
- Musical notes and triads associated with organs and chakras

The individual sounds and frequencies were played to see how they affected autonomic system coherence. These effects were monitored and recorded. Those sounds that placed test subjects in either a medium or high state of coherence were used to create an initial test compilation.

In addition, test volunteers provided subjective feedback as to what sounds they found "pleasant and relaxing", as well as those that disrupted their state of relaxation. The frequencies were then recorded using the human voice creating a melodic compilation that could be used as an independent variable to test against biomarkers that indicate health. This version was tested and refined two additional times before settling on a finalized version. That version included:

- **Bar Chimes** – producing rich harmonic overtones; corresponds with four elements (Earth, Water, Fire, and Air).
- **Tibetan Singing Bowls** – producing a deep field of harmonics, composed of seven metals and the corresponding frequencies; these created with intention in Tibet during ceremony of healing prayers and meditation.
- **Portal Tones** – found in ancient texts, each tone resonates with specific systems or functions: large intestine, spleen, immune system, electrolytes, endocrine, kidney, gallbladder, small intestine, circulation and stomach. Also, near infrasounds (2 – 20 Hz range) for effects on living tissue.
- **Planetary Sounds** – recordings from NASA of planets and the sun, used as a backdrop to create the sense of being part of the bigger picture; the sun frequency as source of life
- **Planetary Harmonics** - Neurobiological Resonance, light, sound and brain wave frequencies (Fiorenza, 2003-2016, p. 1)

- **The Solfeggio Tones** –
    - UT – 396 Hz – turning grief into joy, liberating guilt & fear
    - FA-639 Hz – relationship, connecting with spiritual family
    - SOL – 741 Hz – expression/solutions, cleaning & solving
    - LA-852 Hz – returning to spiritual order
    - RE – 417 Hz – undoing situations & facilitating change
    - MI – 528 Hz – transformation & miracles, repairing DNA
- **Schumann Resonance** – frequency 7.83 Hz and related harmonics
- **Healing and Meditative Mantras** - East Indian, Chinese Warrior & Western sacred mantras
- **Chakras**
    - ♦ **First Chakra** - Saturn theta beats, heartbeat in the womb, frequency 376.3201 Hz, frequency 544.46 Hz frequency of red, wood flute, the note C, toning OooLamVah. (or UhLamDza)
    - ♦ **Second Chakra** - bamboo flute, Anti-Gravity frequency, Pluto frequency 140.25, frequency of orange, the note D, frequency 352 Hz, frequency 606 Hz, E Flat, waterfall, singing, toning OooVamRam
    - ♦ **Third Chakra** - frequency of the Sun 126, Digiridoo, bliss code sound, melodic pad, frequency yellow, frequency 303 Hz, bamboo flute, toning OhRam
    - ♦ **Fourth Chakra** - pad of 44.1, birds, sitar, monolini, rain stick, water drops, F low one, Venus frequency 221.23 Hz,

frequency 442 Hz sound of Venus, toning AhYamHung
- **Fifth Chakra** - singing kung the frequency of Jade, Tibetan throat singing, crickets, throat totem, frequency for Throat Chakra, frequency of Jupiter, Chakra Bowls, the note G, NASA recording of Jupiter, Portal Tones, 505.1 Hz frequency, 384 Hz frequency, the color blue 598.6 Hz, toning EyeHamOm
- **Sixth Chakra and Seventh Chakra** - Tibetan bowls, bells for third eye, Neptune as recorded by NASA, Mercury as recorded by NASA, crystal Pyramids, golden bowls, Himalayan bells, Portal Tones, Bar Chimes, frequencies 606.1 Hz and 707.1 Hz, the notes A and B toning AyeLamShama and EeeOm

- **Triads in Major** – Abbreviated from *Nada Yoga* (Ruiter, 2005, p. 13 - 15)
    - C-major triad – Balanced thinking; head and brain, muscles.
    - G-major triad – Creativity and expression; heart, brain stem, bronchials.
    - D-major triad - Clarity; nervous system, speech, throat, hearing.
    - A-major triad - Liberation; digestion, lymph.
    - E-major triad – Balanced body: heart, circulation, spine and nerves.
    - B-major triad - Unconditional Love; liver, pancreas, spleen, sympathetic nervous system.
    - F sharp-major triad – Unity; blood vessels in the skin, kidney.

- F-major triad - We are all one; grounding effect, edema, balanced metabolism.
- B flat-major triad – Hope and trust; recovery after illness, blood production, muscle coordination.
- E flat-major triad - Supportive of any creative process, bone structure, skin functions, nerve centers in the knees.
- A flat-major triad – Synchronize outer and inner worlds are synchronized, gout and rheumatism.
- D flat-major triad - Catharsis, soothes aggression and anger, bladder, and large intestine. Helpful during stress, after shock, and in allaying deep fears.

- **Triads in Minor**
    - A-minor triad - Open for new developments, spiritual aspirations.
    - E-minor triad - Love for self and the world, soothes depression or hopelessness.
    - B flat-minor triad - Awaking of immortality of the Self.
    - F sharp-minor triad - Deep inner peace for anchoring yourself.
    - C sharp-minor triad – Grounding, stillness, enhances intuitive knowledge.
    - G sharp-minor triad – Comfort, lift above trivial concerns.
    - D minor triad – Open to change, without force.
    - G-minor triad – Confirming desires, inspiration, personal expression.
    - C-minor triad – Accepting Divine guidance.

- ◆ F-minor triad - Love, faith and confidence.
- ◆ B flat-minor triad - Returning to Source, release fear of death.
- ◆ D sharp-minor triad - Feeling free, intuition.

Once the finalized version had been completed, fourteen new subjects ranging in ages from 18 – 75 years were recruited for the study. Again, none of these volunteers were familiar with any of the HeartMath techniques that help build autonomic coherence. Each participant received pre-testing to assess Heart Rate Variability (HRV), and autonomic nervous system coherence using the emWave® Coherence System, (licensed by HeartMath) followed by a basic EDA (Electro-Dermal Analysis using the Avatar Testing System) to assess the energetic functional level of the body's primary meridians. Informed consent was obtained from the new participants, in addition to an intake form assessing variables such as sleep, digestion, pain, energy level, mental focus and emotional issues.

The participants were then asked to sit and listen through headphones to the 30-minute recording of Sayonic Therapy. After listening, HRV, coherence and meridians were retested and recorded for each participant. To determine if the markers would improve using the modality over time, the subjects were then asked to listen to this same recoding every day for two weeks and return for the same tests. Subjects were instructed to listen with headphones in a seated position, at a time they would not be disrupted. They were encouraged to not employ any other meditative techniques during the session, rather simply relax and listen. The project procedure is summarized below.

Procedure for Bioacoustic Frequency Research Project

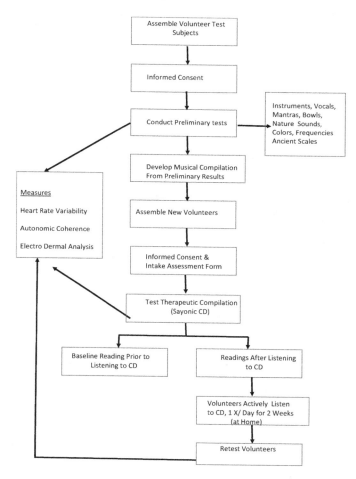

7 RESULTS OF THE RESEARCH

Autonomic System Coherence - Results

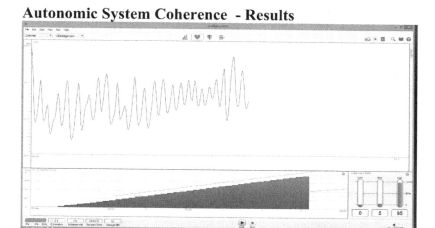

Figure 8 Sample of Individual Coherence Reading - Raw Data

To facilitate a better understanding, the raw data from all of the participants was compiled into graphs below. These charts depict coherence readings before and after one session, then after two weeks of Sayonic Therapy. Findings indicated that the initial session of listening to the final Sayonic Therapy compilation improved autonomic coherence in 80% of the participants.

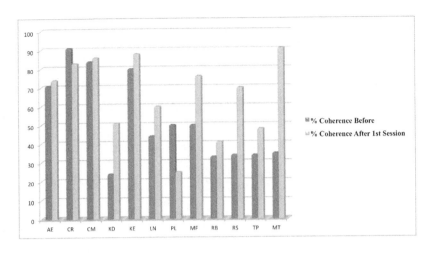

Figure 9. Compilation of All Participants, Percentage of Improvement in Autonomic Coherence after One Session

⁋ The chart above illustrates the percentage of improvement in autonomic coherence after only one session of listening to the final Sayonic Therapy compilation. While 80% of the participants demonstrated overall improvements in coherence, seven of the twelve participants showed a 20% improvement with four of those showing at least a 50% improvement. This increased coherence indicates a corresponding increase in harmony and stability within the dynamic processes of an organism. As proven by research at the HeartMath Institute, this indicates that a shift has taken place toward increased parasympathetic activity, increased heart-brain synchronization and entrainment in the numerous biological systems of the body ("emWave Pro Plus Tour: Overview - Assessments," 2016, p. 20). This corresponds with increases in operating efficiency, where healthful and regenerative processes are enhanced.

A follow-up study was conducted to determine whether or not this coherence could be sustained over time, and would there be an appreciable increase or decrease in coherence from daily use of this therapy. Two of the participants dropped out of the study due to lack of commitment to the project. The two-week follow-up testing indicated that 70% of the participants were able to sustain the improvements in coherence.

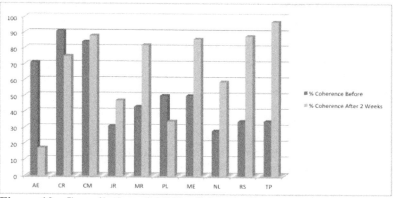

Figure 10. Compilation of All Participants, Percentage Improvements in Autonomic Coherence after Two Weeks

Further, this follow-up study indicated that 60% of the participants were able to sustain improved coherence scores by at least 25% (from their initial state) and that half of the participants improved 50% or more. Again of note, the two participants (anti-depressants and smoking) that did not improve in the first session continued a marked decrease in coherence even after two weeks of therapy.

Figure 7 depicts the results for all three test sessions of the research project. Nine subjects in total participated in all three test sessions. Of the participants that demonstrated improvement after one session, all but one was able to sustain or even improve the levels of higher states of coherence over time.

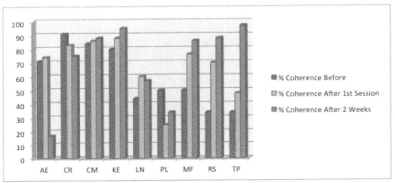

Figure 11. Compilation of All Participants, Percentage Improvements in Coherence - Totals

Research in the public domain has proven that autonomic system coherence and HRV are important biomarkers for health. Optimal levels of both coherence and HRV within an organism reflect healthy function and inherent self-regulatory capacity, adaptability, and resilience. Conversely, instability in these biomarkers is associated with poor health. Numerous research studies have shown that techniques which improve coherence and HRV positively improve both physiological and psychological issues, as well as chronic pain. The Institute of HeartMath has conducted decades of research which demonstrates that utilizing techniques to achieve more coherent states results in establishing new base lines for attaining and sustaining that coherence. The results of this research study indicate that a majority of participants exhibited a higher state of coherence, and half improved their HRV after using Sayonic Therapy. It can be logically deduced that this therapy can assist in improving operating efficiency with in system of the body, enhancing healthful and regenerative processes.

Since it has been proven by HeartMath that a coherent state correlates with a sense of well-being and positive emotions, social, cognitive and physical performance, it would be logical to deduce that Sayonic Therapy would produce a similar response. The subjective feedback from those that participated in this research project reveals that is indeed the case. This will be discussed in more detail later in this book.

Heart Rate Variability - Results

This next chart illustrates Heart Rate Variability in particular, the 1-Minute HRV Deep Breathing Assessment. This test has proven to have a good correlation to a 24-hour vagally mediated HRV, is the most stable short term assessment and adjusts for age-related declines in HRV ("emWave Pro Plus Tour: Overview - Assessments," 2016, p. 14).

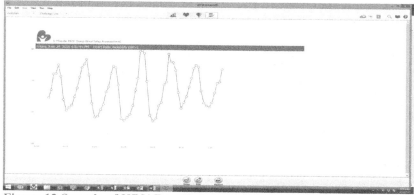

Figure 12 Sample of HRV Raw Data

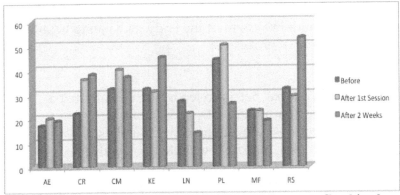

Figure 13. 1-Minute HRV Deep Breathing Assessment, Combined for All Participants

The data shows that HRV had increased in half of the participants, and remained about equal in two others after the initial session. Of the six participants that improved or remained equal, five of those maintained that improvement after two weeks of listening to the Sayonic Therapy compilation. Of those that did not show improvement were the two that were on anti-depressants and smoked heavily. The third participant that showed a decline had been showing higher than normal blood glucose readings, as he kept a daily record. Research shows that HRV can be negatively affected over time by stress levels, sleep patterns, lack of exercise, trauma or injury. The intake forms completed by the participants at the start of the project noted that they were not sleeping well, under a fair amount of stress and exercising very little. In light of that information, this study appears to indicate that the therapy helped modulate the stressor that would have otherwise negatively impacted the readings.

Electro Dermal Analysis (EDA) - Results

In order to observe any possible effects of the bioacoustic frequencies on the vital body (meridians) required a different approach. At this point our technological development, the subtle body meridians cannot be directly measured. However, the vital body can be indirectly observed by measuring the electrical flow (conductance) at various acupuncture points. This conductance or impedance gives us an indication of the energetic health status of the meridian that we are testing. EDA provides a means of indirect measurement of changes occurring within the level of the vital body.

Results of the EDA testing reveal that measurable changes occurred within the subtle energy (Vital) body. These changes are illustrated by the improvement of electrical flow through the meridian channels, an indirect assessment of the biofield. The same meridian points were tested for each participant. However, since subtle body energy is unique to each person, where the meridian imbalances occur will widely vary. All twelve main meridians were measured in addition to the Central and Autonomic Nervous Systems, and the Adrenals. The following chart is a representative example of the raw EDA data gathered for each participant.

Point	Item	Peak	Drop
R Lung CMP		57	1.6
R Large Intestine CMP		62.7	3.5
R Autonomic Nervous System (Paras		59.9	3.4
R Central Nervous System CMP		44.5	0.9
R Circulatory System CMP		49.1	2
R Adrenal Glands - Gonads		40.7	2.6
R Endocrine CMP		49.9	3
R Heart CMP		46.8	3.4
R Small Intestine CMP		51.9	1.7
Pancreas CMP		59.2	1.6
R Liver CMP		58.3	1.4
R Stomach CMP		49.6	4.8
R Gallbladder CMP		59.8	3.2
R Kidney CMP		54.9	2.4
R Urinary Bladder CMP		46.7	1.5
Spleen CMP		44.3	3.8
L Liver CMP		53.7	5.1
L Stomach CMP		50.4	1.6
L Gallbladder CMP		54.9	2.5
L Kidney CMP		57.5	2.1
L Urinary Bladder CMP		60	1.4
L Lung CMP		39.6	1.7
L Large Intestine CMP		51	2.7
L Autonomic Nervous System (Symp		52.8	1.5
L Central Nervous System CMP		50.7	1.9
L Circulatory System CMP		48.5	2
L Adrenal Glands - Gonads		50.5	1.4
L Endocrine CMP		55.3	3.2
L Heart CMP		49.9	2
L Small Intestine CMP		47.8	1.7

Figure 14 Sample EDA Test Data for Bioacoustic Research Project

For this research, the Indicator Drops (ID) were monitored, as these are important markers that indicate an energetic impedance or blockage. To facilitate comprehension of results and to simplify for charting purposes, the readings have been condensed to show only those with an Indicator Drop of 3.0 or greater (a conservative number). The results were charted for each participant on an individualized basis. Some of the participants used the therapy for two weeks, others for one week. The results are considered by participant below. For privacy reasons, each participant is identified by their initials only.

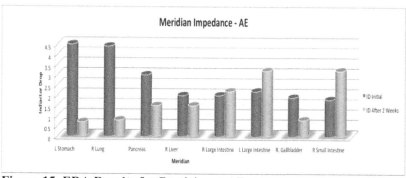

Figure 15 EDA Results for Participant AE

The above chart (Figure 15) depicts the Indicator Drops (ID) for participant AE. The initial elevated ID in the Lung is consistent with her medical diagnosis of asthma, and the Stomach and Pancreas with diabetes and late night eating habits. After two weeks of the Sayonic Therapy, the impedance in these meridians had dropped considerably. However, AE did not show any improvement in coherence and HRV. The EDA is the only form of testing in which she showed some type of movement and improvement. This client is currently taking fourteen prescription medications. After two weeks, she provided this feedback:

> *"I feel much better – a sense of well being. Much calmer and lighter. For the first time in a long time, I've been able to sleep every night without aids. I'm visibly more relaxed – even talking slower."*

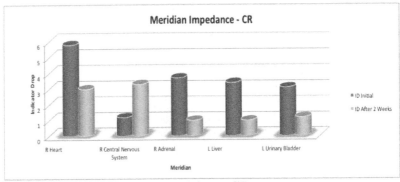

Figure 16 EDA Results for Participant CR

The chart above (Figure 16) provides the data for the Indicator Drops for participant CR. She had marked improvement in vital body energy in all meridians but one. She admits she is a "Type A" person who is constantly on the go. CR did not show much change in coherence (though she ran high at the initial testing), but did show improvement in both HRV and EDA readings.

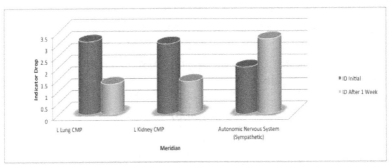

Figure 17 EDA Results for Participant KE

The data in Figure 17 represents the meridian impedance (ID) for participant KE, who has sustained a number of traumatic events in her life. She has been a client for at least a year, and has been actively working to resolve Gastro-intestinal issues as well as the grief and anxiety that had accompanied the trauma. The Lung and Kidney ID's are consistent with her grief and anxiety, respectively. After the Sayonic Therapy study, the homeopathic remedies appeared to have a greater impact on the emotional issues. KE also had improvements in both coherence and HRV. Her feedback is as follows:

"Earlier in the week I had learned some difficult family news which I thought might affect the results of the testing – obviously not; but did start feeling some melancholia on Friday and culminated with a lot of emotional release on Sunday. After speaking with you regarding the test results, which showed significant improvement, I have been listening to the Sayonic CD at night, just before retiring for bed since I have such difficulty getting to sleep. Since starting this, I have been able to fall asleep usually before session is done; a couple of nights had to listen second time but by end of second one was asleep. Each morning I do awaken, feeling refreshed. Some sessions, I zone out and completely lose sense of everything (time/space/surroundings), but I know I haven't fallen asleep. During one session, I was able to release the tears I had been holding back. Thank you for asking me to participate in this Sound Therapy Study."

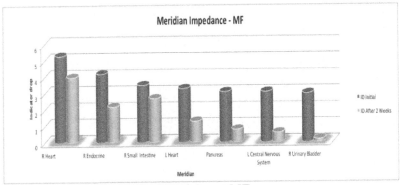

Figure 18 EDA Results for Participant MF

The readings for MF are above in Figure 18. The results indicate improvement in every meridian that had any impedance. She reported a significant drop in blood pressure that is consistent with improvement in the Heart meridians (both left and right), the Endocrine and Central Nervous System. MF's HRV did not vary much, but her coherence score improved considerably. Her feedback is below.

> *"Wow, this is a powerful CD. I'm taking notes. As I put it in today, I felt a lot of old traumas and wounds being pulled out of my heart almost to the point of making it hard to breathe. That is a very good thing. It actually brought me to tears. Blood pressure went down from 197/110 to 140/91. It opened my sinuses. I have wanted to sell my house for two years, but now I am cleaning it and love it. I'm sleeping a little better, and have more energy. After listening to the CD once, my water retention is gone; I was up going to the bathroom all night. Thank you for allowing me to take part in this."*

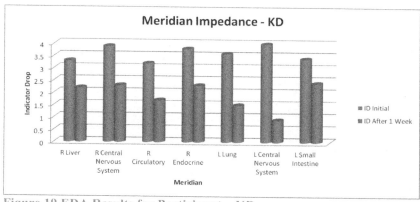

Figure 19 EDA Results for Participant – KD

Participant KD had a number of ID's indicating a fair amount of impedance in the vital body. She reported that she had been under a significant amount of stress with work and family issues, which would be consistent with the number of ID's. As a result, she reported for a follow-up test one week later, but was unable to maintain commitment to the project. With only one week, there was still a measurable improvement.

> *"I have had past trauma. After listening to the music it was like taking a pill but better. The feelings dissipated where the pill just covers it up. It shifted me. I am releasing resentment and anger."*

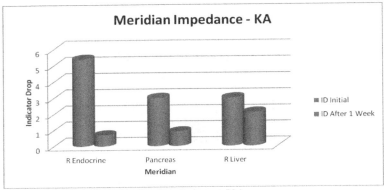

Figure 20 EDA Results for Participant KA

Participant KA had only three Indicator Drops. Her main issues were joint and muscle pain, and inability to have a restful night of sleep due to the pain. She returned in one week for follow-up testing. An improvement was seen in all three but most significant was the reduction in pain and stiffness. She details this in the comment below.

> *"After participating in the healing sound trial, I have experienced an amazing healing. I listened to the healing CD as requested daily for one week. I then listened to it approximately every 2-4 days and sporadically after that time. I had been having horrendous pain radiating from my knee upward and downward and even quite a bit of sciatic nerve pain. It was excruciating to drive and I could barely handle going up and down stairs. The pain was nearly constant and ranged from mild to throbbing. I realized a few days ago that the pain had not been present for a couple of days and I have no more than a random ache. That trend has continued for nearly a week. I am continuing to listen to the CD and watching for more miracles to*

come. Thank you, for all the hard work and study leading up to the scientific trials, and thank you for choosing me to participate."

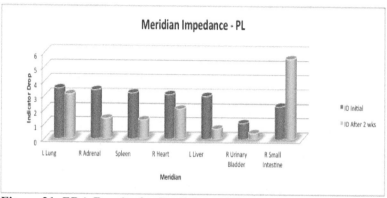

Figure 21 EDA Results for Participant PL

Results for PL are above in Figure 21. This participant is a heavy smoker. While showing no improvement in either coherence or HRV, there is indication that the meridians are being affected positively by the Sayonic Therapy. There is some improvement in all but one meridian; the Small Intestine had an increase in energy blockage.

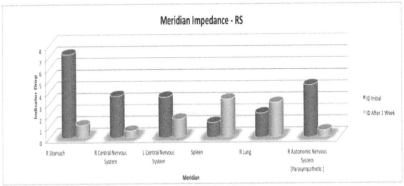

Figure 22 EDA Results for Participant RS

Figure 22 depicts the reading for participant RS. At the initial testing session, RS mentioned that she would return after the study to seek assistance for her digestive distress. This is reflected in her initial readings for the Stomach and Autonomic (Parasympathetic) Nervous system. She was so taken by the music, she listened to the CD at least four times a day and returned after one week for a follow-up. She reported that she felt much improvement in her digestive issues and stomach upsets, as is reflected by the improvements in the Stomach, Autonomic, and both side of the Central Nervous System.

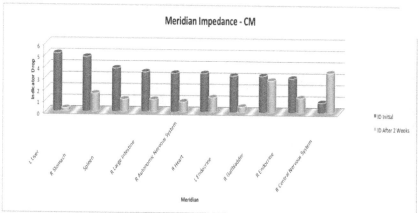

Figure 23 EDA Results for Participant CM

Figure 23 illustrates the results for participant CM. She began the study with ID's in a number of meridians, indicating fair amount of energy impedance through the vital body. After two weeks listening to Sayonic Therapy, she showed marked improvements in eight of the ten meridians. Initial readings for coherence and HRV were very positive and remained through the study. Her feedback is as follows:

> *"The first session, I felt like I wanted to float out of here. I have to be honest, since my two weeks ended, I have not been as diligent in listening, but I am still noticing effects. This morning, I had an epiphany of sorts; it was more of another understanding of how I was brought up/family dynamics. Bottom line, I am noticing a shift. Thanks again."*

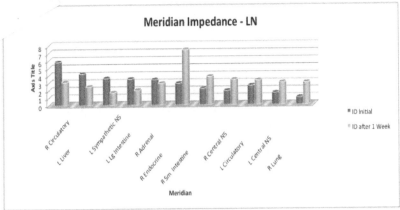

Figure 24 EDA Results for Participant LN

The results for participant LN in Figure 24 reveal a number of interesting points. At the first test session, only five meridians indicated impedance above the designated ID of 3.0. Although all of these areas showed improvement after one week on Sayonic Therapy, another six meridians were developing new issues. During the time of testing, LN had been using a new supplement to address his borderline blood sugar issues. The log of his daily readings showed widely fluctuating blood sugar levels over the past week. The research portion for this participant was halted at that point to address a rebalancing by using supplements and remedies that had been working in the past. On another note, coherence readings for LN did show some improvement, however, HRV readings were decreased after the initial session and after one week. This indicates that the readings obtained during this research project are consistent with published research that correlates diabetes with reduced HRV. He did comment that in addition to experiencing visions while listening, *"It had a very calming effect."*

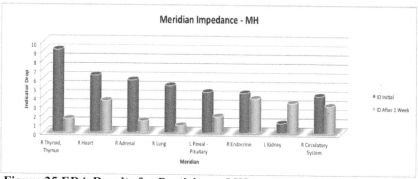

Figure 25 EDA Results for Participant MH

The final participant MH (Figure 24) was able to complete only one week of the trial. Even in this brief time, the EDA reading indicated a marked improvement in several areas. This participant had been subject to extreme amounts of stress over the previous year and reported that she was able to relax and find some measure of peace while listening to the CD.

The above data indicates that improvements in EDA readings (reduced energy impedance in the meridians) proved to be consistent with positive changes and healing as reflected in the mental, emotional and physical symptoms of the individual. Those that did not show improvement correlated with physical issues that are deleterious to health – smoking, excessive pharmaceuticals and elevated blood sugar. Every participant reported improvements in sleep. In addition, participants reported significant improvements in mood and temperament, the ability to handle stress, the capacity to address unresolved emotional pain, and reduction in physical pain.

8 DISCUSSION AND SUMMARY

The results presented in the study illustrate that the beneficial effects of energy medicine can be observed through objective measurement. These effects can be measured in the physical body by measuring the biomarkers of HRV and autonomic coherence. These tests involve the use of electromagnetism, so are perhaps easier to grasp through the model of classical physics. EAV does use electrical flow to determine the health of a meridian, however, it does not measure the actual energy in the meridian. Currently, this capacity lies outside the realm of testing equipment. That the analysis of the human subtle energy field through techniques such as EAV can be more difficult to comprehend from a classical physics standpoint does not mean it should be dismissed. This human subtle energy field, or Biofield, is recognized by the OAM as the existence of "complex of energy fields comprising both electromagnetic forces as well as forces outside those dictated by the laws of classical physics". The results of this research project depict the importance of monitoring this Biofield.

What we can measure is the change of state, the change of energy flow before and after therapy. For readings to be credible, each meridian must be assessed independently. The Indicator Drop is a valuable marker as it depicts the amount of electrical flow that is being impeded in a particular energy channel. Electrical flow impedance corresponds to a change in the concentration of ions in tissues, which corresponds to an accumulation of free radicals and decreased oxygen levels. This eventually results in a change in chemistry. These changes in the Biofield are experienced as changes in feelings and sensations that produce symptoms in the physical body, and corresponding changes in thinking as the mind provides new meanings to these feelings. This change in energy precedes a change in chemistry, thus monitoring energy can be valuable for intervention as well as prevention.

Analysis of the subtle energy body systems, (Biofield) through EAV can provide a wealth of information to practitioners for guiding a client through the healing process. An impedance of energy in the subtle energy field reflects a distortion in consciousness of the physical, mental, emotional or subtle energy realm that is creating a disruption to the integrity of the whole. The disruption can cause a collapse of consciousness in any area of the body. Every physical counterpart to the energy body, that is the organ or tissue correlated to the meridian in the energy body, has a feeling associated with it. When these feeling are suppressed or impeded on any level of the subtle energy field, the energy movement (via the meridians) is suppressed or impeded along with the programs that run the function of the organ. This research project indicated that improvements in the subtle energy readings corresponded to changes in the mental and physical levels. For a few of the participants, changes were being noted on the energy level only, that is, improvements were occurring in the EAV readings but no improvements were being noted in the physiological body through HRV and coherence. Without monitoring the subtle energy body, there is no indication that any changes are occurring. Perhaps the healing effects of other forms of energy medicine are producing a positive impact, yet have been dismissed since these improvements are not being recognized through conventional diagnostics.

Research in the public domain verifies that acoustic frequencies used in Sound Therapy can promote the health of the living organism through a variety of markers. Frequencies from acoustic instruments can improve immune markers such as immunoglobulins, interleukins and natural killer cell, reduce cortisol levels, and affect the electromagnetic field of cells. Fiorenza's research reveals the use of specific frequencies that correspond to color, sound, geometry and planetary harmonic produced positive healing response on physical, emotional and mental levels. Maman's research proves that the human voice produces the most profound healing effects; he believes this is due to the fact that the human voice contains a unique quality - consciousness. Additionally, his research demonstrates that the chromatic scale played in a systematic progression had an effect on cancer cells as the rigid, malignant cells seemed unable to support, "a progressive accumulation of vibratory frequencies." Frequencies generated by electronic equipment do not produce these healing effects. Sound therapies which incorporate electronically generated sounds and frequencies lack the harmonic overtones needed to nourish the subtle bodies. These factors were considered when creating Sayonic Therapy. The "bioacoustic homocord", known as Sayonic Therapy, comprises these and many other frequencies known to be associated with healing, mainly through the use of the human voice, acoustic instruments and a systematic progression of scales and rich harmonic fields. Additionally, this bioacoustic modality was created with the clear, conscious intent to communicate through harmonic resonance the healing vibrational patterns found in nature to place the body in an optimal state for healing. As evidenced by the improvement in several biomarkers – HRV, coherence and meridian impedance - and from the positive subjective feedback, it appears that the Sayonic Therapy did place the body in an optimal state for healing.

Investigative research proves that an optimal level of HRV and high coherence within an organism reflects healthy function and inherent self-regulatory capacity. Coherence signifies a system whose optimal efficient functioning positively affects the ease and flow of life's processes. A coherent state decreases the amount of entropy (disorder) in a system, and the amount of energy necessary for efficient maintenance and repair. The organism moves to a state of centropy, decreasing needed energy input for regulation of life's processes. Through resonance, the healthy frequencies provided through Sayonic Therapy, entrain the homodynamic oscillating systems within the living organism back to a healthy vibrational level. The electromagnetic fields of the body harmonize with the healing frequencies of nature, finding optimal levels of efficiency and performance, thus conserving expenditure of energy.

Techniques that assist in developing and enhancing both HRV and autonomic coherence correlate to improvement in a wide variety of health issues. My research indicated that Sayonic Therapy is a technique that can positively affect both HRV and coherence. Since these markers correlate to improvements in health, and it has been demonstrated here that Sayonic Therapy can positively impact these biomarkers, it can logically be deduced that Sayonic Therapy is a technique that could improve a wide variety of health issues. Results indicate these improvements apply to the physical as well as the subtle energy bodies.

9 CONCLUSION: A SHIFT IN CONSCIOUSNESS

"Concerning matter, we have all been wrong. What we have called matter is energy, whose vibration has been so lowered as to be perceptible to the senses. There is no matter." Albert Einstein

This book discusses the relevance and importance of vibrational therapies as part of a comprehensive system of medicine. It proposes that we are missing a vital dimension in our current model of Western medicine, that is the realm of bioelectromagnetic and subtle energy fields, often termed vibrational or energy medicine. One of the main difficulties for the acceptance of energy medicine is the challenge of demonstrating its beneficial effects through observable and measurable means. Although the recognition and manipulation of energy has been fundamental to healing systems for numerous cultures around the globe, conventional Western medicine still dismisses them as mystical or supernatural, within the realm of pseudoscience. Science, by its very nature, continually seeks to challenge any accepted theory of life and our natural world by attempting to disprove the very theory it just proposed. The true student of science, and by extension medicine, must stand ready to revise their understanding and beliefs independent of emotional attachment, even if it threatens to redefine the very system within which it works. The wisdom of the inextricable link between the physical and the subtle energy bodies is the very basis of healing systems of the ancients and indigenous cultures. Acknowledgment of the energy body and understanding its nature and effects on the chemical or physical body has allowed cultures to survive since the dawn of humanity. If these energy therapies were ineffective, mankind would be a distant memory in the history of life on earth.

Some of these electromagnetic forces, "Veritable Energies", can now be measured and monitored and are gaining acceptance. Yet, those known as "Putative" (subtle energies) have yet to be considered authentic forms of energy. According to Swanson, these energies, which have been overlooked by Western science, constitute a building energy, reversing entropy and restoring order to life. Dr. Yury Kronn proposes that these subtle energies constitute a fifth force that belongs to and acts with the subatomic world. And, Fritz Popp, Herbert Fröhlich and Mae Wan Ho have conducted numerous studies demonstrating the primacy of photonic communication through coherent quantum processes.

Though we do not yet have a means to directly measure these form of "Putative" (subtle) energies, we can still observe their effects through the use of advanced technologies (EDA and SQUID). Homeopathic philosophy states that disturbance of vital energy becomes evident through the manifestation of symptoms on a physical, vital, mental or spiritual level, producing an energetic disorder that is unique to the individual. This is detected by the energy impedances (Indicator Drops) unique to each participant. Also, as the flow of vital energy through the meridians improved through the use of the bioacoustic frequencies, the manifestation of symptoms was markedly decreased as recorded in the biomarkers of HRV and autonomic system coherence and in the reported subjective improvements. This supports Gerber's proposal that the function of vibrational medicine is to interface with primary subtle energy fields, which underlie and contribute to the functional expression of the body.

It has been demonstrated by research in the field of energy medicine that regulation and communication within living organisms can no longer be adequately explained through strictly chemical mechanical means. More than merely nanomolecular concentrations of chemistry, it is electromagnetic frequencies that attenuate cellular receptors facilitating communication within living organisms. It has been demonstrated that coherent fields guide embryonic processes as well as the growth, development and regeneration of cell. Every organ, tissue and cell has its own resonant frequency, which when operating efficiently, resonate and work harmoniously together. When these optimal frequencies are disrupted, impedance in the flow of energy can affect any of the five levels of the body, creating a challenge for our cells to communicate and function properly. The research of Fröhlich has demonstrated that tissue and organs have collective frequencies that regulate cellular processes. When this frequency is altered, loss of coherence ensues that can lead to disease. Hence balance can often be restored by providing the correct or 'healthy' frequency and entraining the oscillations back to coherence. This opens the possibility for sound and bioacoustic frequencies as an option to restore the natural balance.

This work posed the assertion that illness is initiated by imbalances in the energy systems of the body and proposes that methods to detect and correct these imbalances are integral to a comprehensive health system. The results of this study illustrate that detectable changes are occurring on an energetic level, in the meridians, and the bioelectromagnetic fields of the heart and nerves often prior to manifestation in the physical body. Yet, these energetic changes remain undetected by conventional diagnostics. In light of the results of this research, it is the opinion of the author that a comprehensive medical system calls for analysis of the subtle energy systems as well as the physical body.

In summary, the purpose of this research project was three fold. First, to validate the proposed theory that the healing effects of energy medicine could have an objectively measured effect on the energy systems as well as the physical body of the client. The creation of a "bioacoustic homoccord" (Sayonic Therapy), a recorded compilation of specific frequencies and their corresponding deep harmonic fields that resonate with homeostasis provided an independent variable to be used in testing. This allowed for the validation of the proposed theory, providing objective results. *This changes the discussion: the scientific validity of vibrational medicine can be demonstrated; the results of vibrational medicine can be objectively observed and measured using tools that monitor the bioelectromagnetic and subtle energy bodies.*

Second, was to ensure that the results would be measureable and quantifiable in terms of improvements in health. *Results of the present study suggest beneficial effects of energy medicine can be observed through objective measurements of the autonomic system coherence, Heart Rate Variability and electro dermal analysis.* By using a modality of energy medicine in the form of specific, targeted bioacoustic frequencies, the positive impact on biomarkers for health can be observed. It has been determined that all cells, tissues and organs have resonant frequencies that are associated with health. Sayonic Therapy aims to re-introduce sounds that resonate with homeostasis so the cells and tissues will begin to vibrate, through harmonic resonance, restoring a higher vibrational pattern so the body can heal itself. These healthy sounds and patterns represent waves of possibility from which the person can "choose" to collapse a new reality, manifesting a different, healthier state of being.

Third, was to determine if the independent variable, the compilation of specific, targeted bioacoustic frequencies (a therapeutic sound modality trademarked as Sayonic Therapy), could be used as an effective healing modality as a stand-alone therapy or to augment other forms of quantum medicine. *This research establishes that Sayonic Therapy can be an effective form of quantum medicine that empowers the client by consciously engaging them in the healing process.* An unexpected outcome resulting from this study is that this modality, Sayonic Therapy presents an inexpensive, non-invasive therapy to address underserved populations. Irrespective of color or creed, economic or health status, Sayonic Therapy empowers an individual to take an active role in their healing process. Since the creation of the final compilation of the specific bioacoustic frequencies, Sayonic Therapy has been used in conjunction with practices of yoga, massage and chiropractic with very positive results.

For more information regarding the purchase of a Sayonic Therapy CD, contact:

https://store.cdbaby.com/artist/KateHart

REFERENCES

A Sound Structure for the Twenty-First Century. Retrieved from
http://www.soundtravels.co.uk/upload/music/community/pdfs/fabienmaman/cell_experiment.pdf

Abu-Asab, Ph.D., M., Amri, Ph.D., H., & Micozzi, M.D., Ph.D., M. S. (2013). *Avicenna's Medicine: A New Translation of the 11th Century Cannon with Practical Applications for Integrative Health Care.* Rochester, VT: Healing Arts press.

Ahlbom, A., Bridges, J., & Mattsson, M. (2007, March 21). Possible Effects of EMF on Human Health. *Scientific Committee on Emerging and Newly Identified Health Risks (SCENIHR)*, 3 - 63. Retrieved from https://ec.europa.eu/health/ph_risk/committees/04_scenihr/docs/scenihr_o_007.pdf

Beinfield, H., & Korngold, E. (1991). *Between Heaven and Earth: A Guide to Chinese Medicine.* New York, NY: Ballantine Publishing Group.

BioAcoustic Therapy. (). Retrieved from http://www.tophealth.co.za/bioacoustic%20therapy.html

Bioacoustics. (2016). In *Wikipedia*. Retrieved February 15, 2017, from https://en.wikipedia.org/wiki/Bioacoustics

Bioinformative Medicine. (2010). Retrieved from http://www.magnetotherapy.de/fileadmin/download

s/pdfs/E/AMS_Info_Ausland_part_I_to_III_englisch_with_pictures.pdf

Childre, D., Martin, H., & Beech, D. (1999). *The HeartMath Solution*. New York, NY: HarperCollins Publishers.

Chronic Disease Prevention and Health Promotion. (2017). Retrieved from https://www.cdc.gov/chronicdisease/about/prevention.htm

Dekker, J. M., Schouten, E. G., Klootwijk, P., Pool, J., Sweene, C. A., & Kromhout, D. (1997). Heart rate Variability from Short Electrocardiograph Recordings Predict Mortality from All Causes in Middle-aged and Elderly Men. *American Journal of Epidemiology, 145*, 899-908. Retrieved from https://academic.oup.com/aje/article/145/10/899/88911/Heart-Rate-Variability-from-Short?searchresult=1

Drawz, P. E., Babineau, D. C., Brecklin, C., He, J., Kallem, R. R., Soloman, E. Z., ... Appleby, D. (2013, December 14). Heart Rate Variability is a predictor of Mortality in Chronic Kidney Disease; A Report for CRIC Study. *American Journal of Nephrology, 38*, 517-528. Retrieved from https://www.ncbi.nlm.nih.gov/pmc/articles/PMC3920657/

Drouin, P. (2014). *Creative Integrative Medicine: A Medical Doctor's Journey toward a New Vision for Health Care*. Bloomington, IN: Balboa Press.

Eanes, R. (2004). EAV Discussions: Electro-Acupuncture Testing, Electro-Acupuncture According to Dr. Voll. Retrieved from http://eavresource.com/wp-content/uploads/2015/02/EAV-Electro-Acupuncture-Testing-Electro-Acupuncture-According-to-Dr.-Voll.pdf

Edwards, S. (). Frequency as an Intrinsic Healing Factor. Retrieved from http://www.soundhealthoptions.com/frequency-as-intrinsic-healing-modality

Edwards, S. (2001). About SharryEdwardsTM. Retrieved from http://www.soundhealthoptions.com/about

Effect of Sound on Cancer Cells. (). Retrieved from http://www.delamora.life/sound-therapy/cancer-sound-healing/

emWave Pro Plus Assessments. (2016). In *Overview - Assessments*. HeartMath: HeartMath Institute.

Ericcson, A. D., Pittaway, K., & Lai, R. (2003). ElectroDermal Analysis, a Scientific Correlation with Pathophysiology. *Explore!* Retrieved from http://eavresource.com/wp-content/uploads/2015/02/Electro-Dermal-Analysis-study-final-proof.pdf

F., L. M., Tsuei, J. J., & Zhao, Z. (1990). Study of the bioenergetic measurement of acupuncture points for determination of correct dosages of allopathic or homeopathic medicines in the treatment of diabetes mellitus. *American Journal of Acupuncture, 18*).

Fiorenza, N. A. (2003-2016). Planetary Harmonics & Neurobiological Resonances. Retrieved from http://www.lunarplanner.com/Harmonics/planetary-harmonics.html

Gerber, M.D., R. (1998). (1996) *Vibrational Medicine: New Choices for Healing Ourselves.* Santa Fe, NM: Bear & Company.

Goswami, Ph.D., A. (2004). *The Quantum Doctor: A Physicist's Guide to Health and Healing.* Charlottesville, VA: Hampton Roads Publishing.

Goswami, Ph.D., A., Reed, R. E., & Goswami, M. (1993). *The Self-Aware Universe: How Consciousness Creates the Material World.* New York, NY: Penguin Putnam, Inc.

Grigorova, Ph.D., N. G. (2012). *Electro Acupuncture by Voll (EAV) and Homeopathy.* Santa Clara, CA: Milkanan Publishing.

Hahnemann, S. (1982). *Organon of Medicine* (6th Ed.). Blaine, Washington: Cooper Publishing.

Heart Rate Variability Overview. (2017). Retrieved from www.heartmath.com

Ho, M. (2008). *The Rainbow and the Worm: The Physics of Organisms* (3rd Ed.). Hackensack, NJ: World Scientific Publishing Co. Pte. Ltd.

Jaiswal, MBBS, Ph.D, M., Urbina, M.D., M.S., E. M., Wadwa, M.D., R. P., Talton, M.S., J. W., D. Angostino JR, Ph.D., R. B., Hamman, M.D., DRPH, R. F., ... Daniels, M.D., Ph.D, S. (2013).

Reduced Heart Rate Variability Among Youth with Type I Diabetes. *Diabetes Care, 36*, 157-162.

Jelinek, H. F., Imam, H., A-Aubaidy, H., & Khandoker, A. H. (2013, July 26). Association of Cardiovascular Risk Using Non-linear Heart Rate Variability Measures with the Framingham Risk Score in a Rural Population. *Frontiers in Physiology, 4*. http://dx.doi.org/https://dx.doi.org/10.3389%2Ffphys.2013.00186

Kalyuzhny, G. (Volume 4 Number 121, September 2016). The Influence of Electromagnetic Pollution on Living Organisms: Historical Trends and Forecasting Changes. Retrieved from http://www.energytoolsint.com/

Kamp, J. (2016). It's Not So Simple. Retrieved from http://www.vitalforcetechnology.com/uploads/images/downloads/The%20Optimist%20Magazine%20-%20Interview%20with%20Yury%20Kronn%20Spring%202016.pdf

Kaptchuk, T. J. (2000). *The Web That Has No Weaver: Understanding Chinese Medicine.* New York, NY: McGraw-Hill Publshing.

Laszlo, E. (2077) (2007). *Science and the Akashic Field; An Integral Theory of Everything* (2nd ed.). Rochester, VT: Inner Traditions .

Leonhardt, H. (1980). *Fundamentals of Electroacupuncture According to Voll.* C. Beckers Buchdruckerei, Uelzen: Medizinisch Literarische Verlagsgesellschaft mbH.

Lipton, Ph.D., B. H. (2005). *The Biology of Belief: Unleashing the Power of Unconsciousness, Matter & Miracles*. Santa Rosa, CA: Mountain of Love / Elite Books.

Madill, P. (1979, December). Electroacupuncture: A true and legitimate preventative medicine. *American Journal of Acupuncture*.

Madill, P. (1980). Hypoglycemia, Stress and Psychosomatic Illness. *American Journal of Acupuncture, 8*.

Maman, F., & Unsoeld, T. (2016). *The Tao of Sound: Acoustic Healing for the 21st Century* (Second ed.). Malibu, CA: Tama-Do, The Academy of Sound, Color and Movement.

McCraty, Ph.D., R. (2015). *Science of the Heart: Exploring The Role of the Heart in Human Performance, Volume 2*. Boulder Creek, CA: HeartMath Institute.

McCraty, R., Barrios-Choplin, B., Rozman, D., Atkinson, M., & Watkins, A. D. (1998). The impact of a new emotional self-management program on stress, emotions, heart rate variability, DHEA and cortisol. *Integrative Physiological and Behavioral Science, 33*(2), 151-70. Retrieved from https://www.ncbi.nlm.nih.gov/pubmed/9737736

McTaggart, L. (2002). *The Field; The Quest for the Secret Force of the Universe*. New York, NY: HarperCollins Publishers.

Mowry, S. (). Life Transformational Tools: The Ancient Solfeggio Frequencies, the Perfect Circle of Sound. Retrieved from www.miraclesandinspiration.com/solfeggiofrequencies.html

Novotney, A. (2013). Science Watch: Music as Medicine . Retrieved from http://www.apa.org/monitor/2013/11/music.aspx

Oschman, J. L. (2016). *Energy Medicine: The Scientific Basis* (Second ed.). Dover, New Hampshire: Elsevier Ltd.

Oschman, Ph.D, J. L. (2002). *Energy Medicine: The Scientific Basis*. Edinburgh, UK: Elsevier Sciences Limited.

Pischinger, Alfred (2007). *The Extracellular Matrix and Ground Regulation: Basis for Holistic Biological Medicine.* Berkley, CA: North Atlantic Books

Pittaway, K. S. (2002). *Electro Dermal Analysis: Student Handbook.* Livonia, MI: Institute of Natural Health Science.

Pittaway, N.D., Ph.D., K. S. (2001). *Electro Dermal Screening: Student Handbook.* Livonia, MI: Institute of Natural Health Sciences.

Preparation for Childbirth. (2016). Retrieved from http://www.tomatiscalgary.ca/issues-we-impact/preparation-for-childbirth

Rosch, M.D., P. J. (2015). 2014 (Amazon shows 2014 for 2nd ed.) *Bioelectromagnetic and Subtle Energy Medicine* (2nd ed.). Boca Raton, FL: CRC Press.

Rubik, B. (2002, December). The biofield hypothesis: its biophysical basis and role in medicine. *Journal of Alternative and Complimentary Medicine, 8,* 703-717. http://dx.doi.org/https://dx.doi.org/10.1089/1075553 0260511711

Rubik, Ph.D., B., Muehsan, Ph.D., D., Hammerschlag, Ph.D., R., & Jain Ph.D., S. (2015). Biofield Science and Healing: History, Terminology and Concepts. Retrieved from https://www.ncbi.nlm.nih.gov/pmc/articles/PMC46 54789/, Biofield Science and Healing: History, Terminology, and Concepts

Ruiter, D. D. (2005). *Healing Sound Yoga.* Havelte, The Netherlands : Binkey Kok Publications

Sacred Frequencies. (). Retrieved from http://altered-states.net/barry/update205/

Sound Cellular Research. (). Retrieved from http://tama-do.com/roothtmls/cell-research.html

Sound Healing. (November 2005). In *Wikipedia.* Retrieved February, 2017, from https://en.wikipedia.org/wiki/Sound_healing

Sound Healing. (November 2005). In *Wikipedia.* Retrieved February 23, 2017, from https://en.wikipedia.org/wiki/Sound_healing

Swanson, Ph.D., C. V. (2010). *Life Force: The Scientific Basis: Breakthrough Physics of Energy Medicine, Healing, Chi and Quantum Consciousness, Volume II*. Tucson, AZ: Poseidia Press.

Sylver, N. (2011). Rife Therapy Handbook, Appendix C: Healing with Electromedicine and Sound Therapies. Retrieved from http://www.qigonginstitute.org/docs/NenahSylver-Healing%20with%20Electromedicine.pdf

Thayer, J. F., Yamamoto, S. S., & Brosschot, J. F. (2010, May 28, 2010). The relationship of autonomic imbalance, heart rate variability and cardiovascular risk factors. *International Journal of Cardiology, 141*(2), 122-131. Retrieved from www.internationaljournal of cardiology.com/article/S0167-5273(09)01487-91/fulltext

Tomatis, A. A. (1991). *The Conscious Ear*. Barrytown, NY: Stanton Hill Press, Inc.

Tsuei, J. (1996, May/June). Bio-Energetic Medicine: Scientific Evidence in Support of Acupuncture andf Meridian Theory, Part II, The Past, Present and Future of EDSS. *Engineering in Medicine and Biology, Volume 15, Number 3*).

Tsuji, H., Larson, M. G., Venditti, F. J., Manders, E. S., Evans, J. C., Feldman, C. L., & Levy, D. (1996, December 1st). Impact of Reduced Heart Rate Variability on Risk for Cardiac Events . *Circulation, 94*, 2850-2855.

http://dx.doi.org/https://doi.org/10.1161/01.CIR.94.11.2850

Unsoeld, T. (2005, February). FABIEN MAMAN: From Star to Cell - The Way of the Soul. *VISIONS Magazine*. Retrieved from http://tama-do.com/roothtmls/article-visions.html

Voll, R. (1980). The Phenomena of medicine testing in electroacupuncture according to Voll. *American Journal of Acupuncture, 8*).

Wijk, R. V. (2014). *Light in Shaping Life: Biophotons in Biology and Medicine*. Meluna, Geldermalsen, The Netherlands: Ten Brink B.V., Meppel, The Netherlands.

Wuslin, L. R., Horn, P. S., Perry, J. L., Massaro, J. M., & D'Angostino, Sr., R. B. (2015, May). The Contribution of Autonomic Imbalance to the Development of Metabolic Syndrome. *Psychosomatic Medicine, 78*, 474-480. http://dx.doi.org/10.1097/PSY.0000000000000290.

ABOUT THE AUTHOR

Gretchen Weger Snell, PhD, DNM is a clinician and researcher in the field of natural and energy medicine. She utilizes traditional healing methods in combination with the latest technological advances in the field of alternative and natural health care to teach clients to build health naturally. In addition, Dr. Snell is an instructor and faculty member at the Institute of Natural Health Sciences in Farmington, MI. For more information, visit:

http://www.naturalpathconsulting.com

Made in the USA
Middletown, DE
27 June 2020